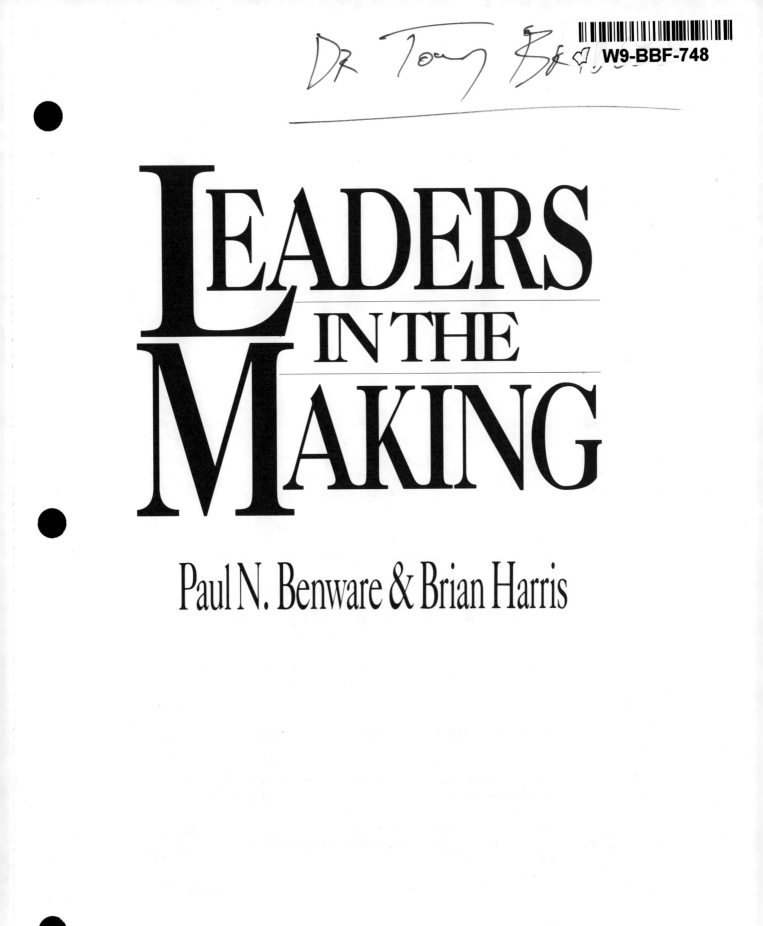

LEADERS
IN THE
MAKING

Paul N. Benware & Brian Harris

MOODY PRESS
CHICAGO

Library of Congress Cataloging-in-Publication Data

Benware, Paul N., 1942-
   Leaders in the making: a workbook for discovering and
developing church leaders / Paul N. Benware and Brian P. Harris.
   p.   cm.
   ISBN 0-8024-4928-X
   1. Christian leadership. 2. Lay ministry—Recruiting.
I. Harris, Brian P.   II. Title.
[BV652.1.B45   1991]
253—dc20   91-13251
                                                                CIP

3 4 5 6 7 Printing/VP/Year 96 95 94

Printed in the United States of America

CONTENTS

FOREWORD

Leadership.

It is the single issue that either makes or breaks the success of ministry. Tragically there is a growing void of effective leadership in many churches and Christian organizations. It's not that we don't have people placed in key positions; it is that key positions are often filled with those who are not qualified or trained to lead.

It has been well said that "leaders are made, not born." Making leaders by training men and women to lead effectively the cause of Christ, therefore, becomes one of the highest priorities of the church.

As a pastor, I was well aware that the making of leaders was vital to the future of the ministry. My frustration, however, was the lack of an effective agenda for grooming leadership. Furthermore, there was the lack of available resources that were organized well and were biblically sound and practical.

One glance at *Leaders in the Making* and I felt a sense of regret that it has not been available throughout the last several decades. My regret was soon balanced by my enthusiasm that now pastors and church leaders will have this tool. It is both profound in its teaching and practical in its application.

The fact that Dr. Paul Benware and Pastor Brian Harris have used this material in their own church settings adds validity. This is not just another idea cast to frontline generals from ivory-tower word processors.

The genius of this work is that it deals with more than mere method and skill. It begins with the most crucial issue of leadership, which is not a man's performance but rather a man's character. Basic principles on the "inner life" are explained, providing lifelong disciplines of growth and godliness.

The target of growth as a church leader—scriptural qualifications—is well established in the clear and convicting section "Biblical Ideals."

Leaders must have a heart for the cause they are leading. Needless to say the pastor's cause, first and foremost, is winning lost people for our Lord and Savior, Jesus Christ. The section on evangelism will put leaders into the frontline trenches with new commitment—and with good theology that will give them confidence and strength.

The unique idea in Christ's kind of leadership is that His leaders are to be servants. In the section on "shepherding," this unique perspective is not only clearly explained but practically outlined in terms of what it actually means to be a servant-leader.

You will share my enthusiasm as you look through this material. It is clear, understandable, and significant in its depth and authenticity. You will find this is more than just another theoretical discipleship tool: it is usable. It will have great impact on those who want to grow in their capacities to serve Jesus Christ effectively.

JOSEPH M. STOWELL, III, PRESIDENT
Moody Bible Institute

PREFACE

Leaders are to lead. Simply occupying the position of elder, deacon, or chairman of a committee does not make a person a leader. There are some in leadership positions who are simply managers of the status quo; they provide very little leadership. The church is faced with the need for good leaders, but often quality leaders are nowhere to be found. It is well known that soft societies and sickly homes do not normally produce good leaders. As a result, the church finds as never before that it must give much greater attention to discovering, developing, and training of leaders. Churches that fail to cultivate leaders will probably face a shortage in leadership in the near future. This workbook is designed to be a tool in the strategic task of leadership development.

This training book is divided into four study areas, with a total of twenty sessions. These areas of study are not necessarily dependent on one another and could, therefore, be studied in a different order.

Another important feature of this workbook is the integral use of five other books. They will stimulate new ideas and provide helpful insights into the respective study areas with which they are used. The four study areas and their associated reading sources are listed.

> Study Area 1: The Inner Life of Church Leaders
> Gordon MacDonald, *Ordering Your Private World*
> Oswald Sanders, *Spiritual Leadership*, 3d ed., rev.

> Study Area 2: The Biblical Ideals for Church Leaders
> Gene Getz, *The Measure of a Man*
> Oswald Sanders, *Spiritual Leadership*, 3d ed., rev.

> Study Area 3: The Evangelistic Work of Church Leaders
> Charles Ryrie, *So Great Salvation*

> Study Area 4: The Shepherding Ministries of Church Leaders
> Michael Slater, *Becoming a Stretcher Bearer*

Even though we live in an incredibly fast paced society and generally insist on doing things quickly, growth of any kind cannot be hurried or forced. Spiritual growth is no exception. It simply takes time to read, think, pray, and evaluate. This book takes this process into consideration. The group study depends on the personal reading, careful study, and thoughtful meditation of each individual. It would be fruitless and frustrating to try to go through this workbook on a weekend retreat. Each church will want to adapt these study areas to its own unique situation. However, several possible ways to use this are:

1. Meet every other week, starting in September and ending in May. Each meeting would last for about two hours.
2. Meet once a month for nine months. An extended period of time of about four hours would be needed—possibly on a Saturday morning.
3. Meet less frequently between the months of September and May. Carry over the study into the following fall.
4. Run two study groups concurrently each fall and spring. An individual is free to elect the study area of greatest interest or need to him. In due time, each person will rotate through all four of the study areas.

The basic Bible text for this book is the *New International Version* (NIV). Bible quotations from any text other than the NIV will be designated by accompanying abbreviations as follows: King James Version (KJV), *New King James Version* (NKJV), *New American Standard Bible* (NASB), *Living Bible* (LB), *The Amplified Bible* (Amp.), or *New Testament in Modern English* (Phillips).

INTRODUCTION:
THE BIBLICAL TRAINING OF CHURCH LEADERS

As we begin this training program, it is important that we build on a solid, biblical foundation. Certain scriptural presuppositions need to be mentioned, since many of the subsequent sessions will be built on them. There are four foundations of an equipping ministry:

I. THE LOCAL CHURCH IS TO BE A TRAINING BASE FOR MINISTRY (EPHESIANS 4:11-13)

Although schools, seminars, and the mass media can all be helpful in training individuals, we must understand that the church is the primary place for that ministry of equipping believers for serving the Lord Jesus Christ.

Ephesians 4:11-13 is not an obscure passage of Scripture. Although well-known by evangelical Christians, it is often misunderstood or ignored. Far too often Christians in the church see the paid pastors as *the* ministers, while the congregation is seen as the recipients of their ministry. However, this passage is clear that those who were leaders (apostles, prophets, evangelists, pastors, and teachers) were given to the church to prepare the individual members for ministry.

> God never intended for the members of the body of Christ to become dependent on one leader to do "the work of the ministry" . . . God did not even intend for several leaders to do the work of the ministry. Rather, He intended for the whole church to do this work. It is a responsibility of church leaders to equip the saints to serve![1]

When Ephesians 4:11-13 is studied, several key words become apparent. The pivotal word in this passage is "prepare." It is rendered in other translations as "perfecting" (KJV), "equipped" (LB), "equipping" (NASB), "the perfecting and full equipping" (Amp.) and "properly equipped" (Phillips). W. E. Vine defines the Greek word *katortisomos* as "a fitting or preparing fully."[2]

Ephesians, probably more than any other New Testament book, presents God's blueprint for the church. In Ephesian 4, Paul lists the provisions of Christ for the ongoing growth of the church. One of these provisions is the bestowal of gifted leaders. These leaders are to organize, train, and equip the church members for service. These members are converts from a wide variety of backgrounds and possessing a great diversity of attitudes and abilities. Out of this chaos and disorder is to be brought purposeful and functioning order. As the church is trained and organized, it is then released for service.

As the church is prepared or equipped for service, three results are all closely dependent on one another. The church body is "built up," achieving "unity"

---

1. Gene Getz, *Sharpening the Focus of the Church* (Wheaton: Victor, 1984), p. 81.
2. W. E. Vine, *Expository Dictionary of New Testament Words* (London: Oliphants, 1963), 2:175.

and becoming "mature." The main thrust is that the church must be equipped for ministry to reach its fullest potential. Two assumptions in these verses are: (1) each believer has a specific gift or function in the church, and (2) the church is hindered if all are not equipped and functioning (v. 7).

An important word in this text is the word translated "built up." In its literal usage it is used in reference to the building of a house. In the New Testament it refers figuratively to spiritual growth. Just as there are various steps and processes in building a home, likewise, there are steps in the process of spiritual growth.

Another pivotal word in the text is "unity." The word simply means "oneness." This oneness is in the faith and knowledge of Christ. An absence of division in the church is an indication of oneness and maturity.

Ephesians 4 leaves little doubt that the church is to be the training base for ministry, providing for the growth and maturity of individuals, as well as the church as a whole.

A QUESTION TO CONSIDER: What are some dangers that face a church when it simply hires paid professionals to do the work of the ministry and does not train the people for ministry?

II. THE ELDERS OF THE CHURCH ARE CALLED TO EQUIP PEOPLE FOR MINISTRY (2 TIMOTHY 2:2)

Along with the truths of Ephesians 4:11-13, the apostle Paul's statement to Timothy (who was apparently the pastor-teacher of the Ephesian church) is significant.

> And the things you have heard me say in the presence of many witnesses entrust to reliable men who will also be qualified to teach others (2 Tim. 2:2).

This ministry of multiplication of leaders is God's way of providing for the needed guidance and stability of the church. Proved men are to train others to minister, and these in turn train others.

If the church is to be the training base for ministry, then someone must take the initiative in training, and that is the responsibility of the elders and often, more specifically, the pastor. For the past century, many churches and pastors have viewed the role and function of the pastor improperly. He is seen as *the* minister, the president of the corporation, the benevolent dictator, the chaplain who renders service to his clients, the paid performer, the professional Christian. All of these views stand in opposition to the teachings of Scripture. "Every Christian leader must constantly strive to keep his people from becoming overly dependent on him. He must strive to equip the saints to minister to each other and keep their primary loyalty centered on Christ."[3]

It is important, of course, to provide godly models for people to follow. Such visible, personal examples are essential for growth in the lives of believers. But the

3. Getz, *Sharpening the Focus*, p. 120.

leaders must strive to get others trained and involved in ministry. This equipping of others for service is the biblical model of pastoral leadership.

A QUESTION TO CONSIDER: What are some dangers that face a church when there is one dominant leader in that church? _____

_____

_____

III. THERE IS TO BE A PLURALITY OF LEADERSHIP IN THE LOCAL CHURCH (ACTS 14:23)

This presupposition builds on the previous one. The evidence of the New Testament strongly favors a plurality of elders in each local church. For example, in Acts 14:23 the statement is made that "Paul and Barnabas appointed elders for them in each church and, with prayer and fasting, committed them to the Lord, in whom they had put their trust."

Note that Paul and Barnabas appointed elders, not just one elder. The early church, first in Jerusalem and later in other cities, began with multiple leadership. Even Paul, as he planted churches, did so as part of a ministry team. The following are some New Testament references to multiple leadership.

> Acts 13:2. The church in Antioch had *prophets* and *teachers*.
> Acts 20:17. Paul called for the *elders* from Ephesus to come to him.
> Philippians 1:1. The letter is addressed to the *elders* and *deacons*.
> Titus 1:5. Titus was sent to appoint *elders* in every town.
> 1 Peter 5:1-2. Peter, as an elder, addresses his fellow *elders*.
> James 5:14. In the time of need, the *elders* should be called to help.

Everywhere in the New Testament Scriptures we find ministry being done by groups of people. In the New Testament we do not find the "lone ranger" model of ministry that is often seen in churches today. The church is to be governed, shepherded, and taught by a plurality of leaders. There is greater wisdom with a plurality of elders, and many dangers and problems that accompany leadership are reduced.

A QUESTION TO CONSIDER: What dangers and problems that accompany leadership would be reduced or avoided by having a plurality in the leadership of the local church? _____

_____

_____

IV. BIBLICAL LEADERSHIP IS A POSITION OF SERVANTHOOD RATHER THAN LORDSHIP (MARK 10:42-45)

There are a number of contrasts between a biblical concept of leadership and the view of leadership that is commonly found in the political, business, or social areas. Whereas some other organizations may talk about servanthood, it is only in the church that it can become a reality. Scriptures teach the concept of the leader as a servant. Key among those passages are Mark 10:35-45 and John 13:13-17. These provide an excellent summary of Christ's teaching on this subject. Some of the truths found in these Scriptures are: (1) the servant-leader concept stands in opposition to the idea of leadership in the world; (2) greatness is shown through a willingness to serve others, not by how many serve us; (3) God is the one who grants places of leadership to people; (4) leadership may involve hardship and suffering; (5) a wrong view of leadership will lead to disharmony within the Body of Christ; and (6) biblical leadership leads to God's blessing.

A QUESTION TO CONSIDER: In what ways might a servant attitude be evidenced in a leader?

_____

_____

_____

_____

STUDY AREA 1
The Inner Life of Church Leaders

The goal of this study area is to remind elders, deacons, and potential leaders that the most important ingredient for effective Christian leadership is the inner life. Gordon MacDonald states, "If my private world is in order, it will be because I am convinced that the inner world of the spiritual must govern the outer world of activity."[1]

TEXTS FOR THIS STUDY AREA:

Gordon MacDonald. *Ordering Your Private World.* Nashville: Oliver Nelson, 1984.

Oswald Sanders. *Spiritual Leadership.* 3d ed., rev. Chicago: Moody, 1994.

---

1. Gordon MacDonald, *Ordering Your Private World,* p. 12.

THE INNER LIFE OF CHURCH LEADERS
SESSION 1:
SPIRITUALITY AND CONTROL

PREPARATORY ASSIGNMENTS:

1. In preparation for this session, read pages 7-26 in *Ordering Your Private World*, and briefly answer the following questions.
   According to Gordon MacDonald, what is the basic principle that must be built upon in ordering the inner life? _____

   _____

   _____

   What is the "sinkhole syndrome"? _____

   _____

   _____

   Why is so little attention given to the inner life? _____

   _____

   _____

   If the "bridge" is the control center of life, who must control the bridge? _____

   _____

   _____

2. Also read chapter 10 in *Spiritual Leadership*, and answer the following questions.
   According to Oswald Sanders, what is indispensable for spiritual leadership?

   _____

   _____

   And why is this true? _____

   _____

   What is the result of electing elders and deacons without this requirement?

   _____

   _____

   _____

   What is a one word definition for being filled with the Spirit? _____

The filling of the Spirit is absolutely essential for serving effectively as an elder or deacon. It is something that is expected and required for those who would lead the flock of God. Since the filling of the Spirit is vital to leadership, it is important to discuss this early in this training time. Two questions need to be discussed: (1) What is the filling of the Spirit? and (2) How am I filled with the Spirit?

I. WHAT IS THE FILLING OF THE SPIRIT?

Ephesians 5:18 is a key passage on the filling of the Holy Spirit, summarizing this ministry: "And do not get drunk with wine, for that is dissipation, but be filled with the Spirit."

A. THE CONTRAST

In this verse, the filling of the Spirit is contrasted with drunkenness. That seems strange until the meaning is understood. To be drunk with wine is to be controlled, or dominated, by alcohol. Drunkenness is sometimes referred to as being "under the influence." To be filled with the Holy Spirit is to be under His influence, or control.

B. THE COMMAND

Believers are commanded to be filled with the Spirit. Whenever something is a command two truths are clear; it is neither an option, nor is it something that automatically takes place. Believers are to act upon this divinely given order.

C. THE TENSE

The present tense tells us that the filling of the Spirit is a continuous, progressive experience. So Christians are to "keep on being filled."

D. THE ASPECTS

Ephesians 5:18 describes the *progressive* aspect of filling. As we become more and more controlled by the Holy Spirit in the various areas of life, sin and selfishness loose their grip (progressive sanctification). This is the lifetime experience of the believer.[1] The New Testament also speaks of the *crisis* aspect of filling (see Acts 2:4; 4:8, 31). These were unique occasions where, in response to prayer, special ability (boldness, power to witness or speak) was given to meet a difficult or unique situation. It was temporary, for the moment only. Also, it is interesting to note that these believers did not pray to be filled but were controlled by the Spirit in response to their prayers for boldness or power to minister effectively in difficult circumstances.

E. THE DISTINCTION

Confusion about the two ministries of the Spirit, baptism and filling, often prevails. They are not to be equated, but understood as two distinct ministries. The baptism of the Spirit takes place at the time of the believer's salvation. Baptism is the

---

1. Brian Harris believes that the progressive aspect of filling becomes a significant reality only after a believer makes a conscious decision to submit to the lordship of Jesus Christ. Without that decision, filling is slow and erratic at best, or nonexistent at worst.

common experience of all believers (see 1 Cor. 12:13). Baptism is that act of the Spirit whereby we are placed into union with Christ, into His Body. It is not something that is commanded. It is something that automatically takes place, and nowhere is a believer exhorted or commanded to seek Spirit baptism.

A QUESTION TO CONSIDER: What are several contrasts between filling and baptizing?

_____

_____

_____

F. THE EVIDENCES

At times, the best way to describe a Christian experience is to list its characteristics when it is operational in the life of a believer. There are numerous evidences of the Spirit's control of a believer's life.

A spirit of joy and praise (Eph. 5:19-20)
An attitude of submission (Eph. 5:21)
Expression of the fruit of the Holy Spirit (Gal. 5:22-23)
A godly lifestyle based on the Word of God (1 Pet. 1:16; 1 Thess. 4:3)
Spiritual gifts recognized and put to work (Eph. 4:7-16)
A burden to see unbelievers saved (Matt. 28:19-20)
A consistent devotional life (Ps. 119:9, 11; Rom. 15:4; Acts 10:2)
A desire to obey Christ at any cost (1 Sam. 15:22; Acts 5:29)

II. HOW TO BE FILLED WITH THE SPIRIT

It is interesting to note that the New Testament does not give a neat, concise formula for being filled with the Spirit. Although such a formula does not exist, the Bible does say a great deal about the subject, and its teachings can be summarized in three terms: understanding, submission, and faith.

A. UNDERSTANDING

Certain basic truths need to be understood. We must know that we are saved; that God's Holy Spirit dwells within us; and that God expects us to be filled with the Spirit. These are foundational truths. The key to Spirit control is Word control. We must know God's standards and expectations before we can submit to Him. For example, the Spirit cannot control the area of finances if we do not know what God has said about money and material possessions. As we learn more and more about God's truth in the area of money and submit to Him, the Spirit progressively gains greater control in that area of life. There can be no control where there is no knowledge of God's Word. It is imperative, therefore, that we consistently study the Scriptures in order to understand God's truth as it addresses the various areas of life.

B. SUBMISSION

Submission means to renounce our own way and seek above all else to submit to Christ as the Lord. It is allowing Him to rule over the various areas that make up our lives. If He is not ruling, then we are. And the essence of sin is self-will. Submission involves the confessing and repenting of all known sin. Sin prevents the working of the Holy Spirit in our lives. We cannot be filled with sin and the Spirit at the same time. Submission also involves our yielding to God and His will. Yield means to place yourself at the disposal of God. It is saying, "God, I'm yours, use me!" We are to submit, recognizing that as we come to know and understand God's truth we will need to submit in other areas as well. We should be more controlled by the Spirit today than we were a year ago, because we have learned more of the Word of God and sumbitted ourselves to the standards of the Word. It is important to note that the filling of the Spirit is not an irrational or strictly emotional experience. Rather, it is an act of the will and intellect, obeying the commands of God's Word.

C. FAITH

After we understand these truths that God wants us to know and have submitted our wills to God, we must walk in faith. When we are yielded to God and to His will, we are "being controlled" by the Spirit. The filling of the Spirit means not getting more of the Spirit, but rather the Spirit's getting more of us. Now we are to act on that truth and live with full assurance that God has and is filling us, that we are under His control. Paul put it this way in Romans 6:11: "Count yourselves dead to sin, but alive to God." To "count" is an act of faith. It is not make-believe or pretense, but rather acting on God's promise.

SUMMARY

Several truths related to the filling of the Spirit must be recognized:

The filling of the Spirit is not a matter of feeling but of faith based on the facts of God's Word.

Filling does not mean that we are perfect and sinless. Sin is still a reality, and we must be prepared to deal with it.

The filling of the Spirit is not a once-for-all event but a continuous process.

Filling means controlling. It is the Spirit's getting more of us, not we getting more of the Spirit.

As an elder or deacon or potential leader, it is important that you deal seriously with this issue of the filling of the Spirit. Without it your leadership will be based on your own abilities and not on the Spirit's power. And your own abilities will soon fail.

THE INNER LIFE OF CHURCH LEADERS

SESSION 2:
ROUTINE AND DEVOTIONS

Our personal relationship with the Lord is critical to the spiritual well-being of all believers, including those who lead. The devotional life of the leader cannot be neglected without its hurting his own life and his ability to lead God's people.

PREPARATORY ASSIGNMENTS:

1. The life of the Lord Jesus was the perfect model of a strong, healthy devotional life. Read the following passages, and list the principles and characteristics of His devotional life that you discover. Then make an application to your devotional life.

Luke 2:40-52 _____

_____

Luke 3:21-22 _____

_____

Mark 1:35-39 _____

_____

Luke 5:15-16 _____

_____

Luke 6:12-16 _____

_____

Matthew 14:3-13 _____

_____

Matthew 26:36-46 _____

_____

Luke 23:32-34; 44-46 _____

_____

Hebrews 4:14-16; 7:23-26 _____

_____

2. After reading chapter 11 in *Spiritual Leadership*, answer these questions.
   How do you feel about your prayer life? Why? _____

   _____

   _____

   How did an extra load of work affect Martin Luther's prayer life? _____

   _____

   According to Oswald Sanders, there is no way to learn to pray except by _____

   _____

   What does praying "in the Spirit" mean? _____

   _____

   _____

3. Read pages 115-58 in *Ordering Your Private World,* and answer these questions.
   What metaphor does Gordon MacDonald use to describe our devotional life?

   _____

   Why is that a good metaphor? _____

   _____

   What privileges do we lose when we neglect prayer? _____

   _____

   _____

   What does MacDonald mean by the term "internalized"? _____

   _____

   _____

   What are your greatest hindrances to prayer? _____

   _____

   _____

   From these pages, what did you learn that can be of help in improving your
   devotional life?

   _____

   _____

   _____

I. HELPS FOR YOUR DEVOTIONAL LIFE

The question arises: How can I develop a vital and meaningful devotional life? No magical formula exists, but the following are given as practical suggestions to help improve your devotional life.

A. WHERE DO I HAVE MY DEVOTIONS?

Jesus in Matthew 6:6 says: "But when you pray, go into your room, close the door and pray to your father." As we learned from our study of Jesus' prayer life, He modeled this: "But Jesus often withdrew to lonely places and prayed" (Luke 6:16). I am convinced that one of the most important steps one can take to improve his/her prayer life is to establish a prayer closet, a place to be alone with the Lord. Andrew Murray, in *The Believer's School of Prayer,* says, "He (God) wants each one to choose for himself the fixed spot where Jesus can daily meet him" (p. 24). Find or create a prayer closet that is available to you on a daily basis. It may be a spare room, the basement workshop, the dining room table, or perhaps a literal closet. It should be your place to meet your Lord. You may have to rise early or stay up late to find such a place in your home. In warmer weather, head outdoors for prayer retreats. Reserve your prayer closet, and inform your family of your intentions. In addition, help your wife and children develop their prayer closets.

B. WHEN DO I SCHEDULE MY DEVOTIONAL LIFE?

Choose a time when you are the most alert and receptive to God's still small voice. It should be a time when you feel the least distracted or when there are the least opportunities for interruptions. For some, this is early morning; for others, late at night. Experiment, and pick the time that is best for you.

This time should be reserved daily. Mark it in your daily appointment calendar. Experienced prayer warriors recommend that you begin with five to ten minutes per day for your quiet time. Then gradually increase your time for as long as you have available for prayer each day. Thirty minutes to one hour of devotional reading and prayer each day would be a worthy goal for a spiritual leader.

In addition to this main devotional "meal" of the day, take time for devotional "snacks." Following are just a few suggestions:

Carry a New Testament or Christian book to read while waiting in line or for appointments.

Send up silent prayers for those you meet or associate with during the day.

Plan your noon lunch time to spend one-half of the time eating and one-half of the time reading or praying.

Plan times to pray with your wife and children.

Listen to Christian music, sermons, and teaching or the Scripture on cassette as you drive.

Develop a habit of silently talking about every aspect of your day with your Lord. Paul called this praying without ceasing.

Plan expanded prayer retreats for several hours or a day.

C. HOW DO I STRUCTURE MY DEVOTIONAL LIFE?

1. *Prayer pattern.* There are several patterns for prayer: Matthew 6:9-13 and Luke 11:2-4 give what is referred to as the Lord's Prayer. The Lord's purpose in giving this prayer was to provide a formula or model for prayer. It was not given as a prayer to recite verbatim. This model prayer can be divided into a simple two-step pattern: praise and petition.

Praise relates to the nature of God; that is, worshiping Him for who He is. Praise involves our: (1) relationship to God; "Our Father in heaven," (2) our reverence for God; "Hallowed be your name," and (3) our resignation before God; "Your kingdom come, your will be done, on earth as it is in heaven."

Petition refers to the requests we make of God. Three types of requests are given: (1) a request for physical provision; "Give us today our daily bread," (2) a request for pardon; "Forgive us our debts as we also have forgiven our debtors," and (3) a request for spiritual protection; "And lead us not into temptation, but deliver us from the evil one."

MacDonald in chapter 13 lists a three-step pattern of prayer: adoration, worship of God, and intercession.

Another is the ACTS formula: adoration, confession, thanksgiving, and supplication. Perhaps you have a prayer pattern with which you are comfortable. The specific pattern is not so important as the fact that we remember that prayer should do two basic things: worship God and present our needs to Him.

2. *Study.* Along with prayer, a major portion of devotional time must be given over to the reading and studying of God's Word and the devotional writings of other men and women of God. Prayer is man speaking to God; study and meditation is God speaking to man. A college professor once said to me that "leaders are readers," and I have come to realize the importance of that statement.

As spiritual leaders, we must be men of "The Book." Develop a Bible reading schedule that takes you through all the books of the Bible.

In addition to Scripture reading, it can be helpful to read a few pages or a chapter from a devotional book. Read both contemporary and classical books. Suggested authors are A. W. Tozer, Andrew Murray, E. M. Bounds, Charles Swindoll, Francis Schaeffer, A. B. Simpson, and Philip Keller.

For further reading, see: *Ordering Your Private World* (chap. 9) and *Spiritual Leadership* (chap. 13).

3. *Meditation.* Psalm 1:2 in describing the blessed man says: "But his delight is in the law of the Lord and on his law he meditates day and night." A vital part of our devotional life is meditation. Do not be afraid of that term. This is not the meditation of Zen, yoga, or TM. Richard Foster, in his book *Celebration of Discipline* says: "Meditation has always stood as a classical and central part of Christian devotion, a crucial preparation for and adjunct to the work of prayer."[1] He goes on to differentiate between Christian and Eastern meditation: "Eastern meditation is an attempt to empty the mind, Christian meditation is an attempt to empty the mind in order to fill it."[2] Christian meditation is filling the mind with the Word of God and contemplating its meaning and application to one's life. The word "meditate" is closely related to

1. Richard Foster, *Celebration of Discipline* (San Francisco: Harper, 1978), p. 14.
2. Ibid., p. 15.

"ruminate." Ruminate is what a cow does as it "chews the cud." It fills its stomach quickly and later, at its leisure, brings its food back up to further chew it. As you read and study God's Word and other reading, take time to meditate.

For further reading, see: *Celebration of Discipline*, chapter 3, and *Ordering Your Private World*, chapter 11.

4. *Journaling*. In chapter 11 MacDonald does an excellent job of urging his readers to keep a journal as part of their devotional life. This can be extremely beneficial. In a journal, list daily activities, joys, and frustrations, meaningful Scripture verses and quotes from devotional books, prayers, and other matters that impact you.

5. *Prayer and Fasting*. Fasting has gone out of style in today's church, and this is a great loss. For the believer, fasting, as meditation, is not just an Eastern practice— it is a biblical concept. Matthew 6:16 says, "when you fast." Scripture does not command one to fast, but it does imply that the believer will.

Fasting is the missing of a meal or meals to devote that time to prayer, study, and/or meditation. Many times believers engage in fasting to seek God's direction for a major decision or to lay a special prayer concern before Him. Seriously consider the adoption of prayer and fasting as part of your devotional life.

II. EVALUATION OF YOUR DEVOTIONAL LIFE

The following questionnaire will help you evaluate your devotional life and perhaps show areas that need strengthening or improvement.

A. How much do you pray in any given week? _____

   When do you pray? _____

   _____

B. Do you pray with your wife and children? _____

   When? _____

C. Do you have a Bible reading plan? _____

   What is it? _____

   _____

D. What devotional books have you read in the past year? _____

   _____

   _____

E. What percentage of your prayer time do you spend in

    Adoration (worship)   _____%

    Confession   _____%

    Thanksgiving   _____%

    Supplication   _____%

    —for yourself   _____%

    —for others   _____%

       TOTAL   _____%

F. In what areas does your devotional life need improvement? _____

_____

_____

G. List one goal for improving your devotional life and an action plan to achieve it.

    GOAL: _____

_____

_____

    ACTION PLAN: _____

_____

_____

_____

_____

SESSION 3:
FAMILY AND HOME

The ministry of an elder or a deacon is a public ministry, and people are able to observe those many outward acts of service. However, as we have already seen, the inner life of the leader is just as important. A leader can hide much of his life from many people, but he cannot hide the true character of his inner life from his family. Before he can be a spiritual leader in the church, the elder or deacon must be the spiritual leader in the home.

PREPARATORY ASSIGNMENT:

One of the requirements of Scripture for an elder is that he must "manage his own household well" (1 Tim. 3:4). It is logical as well as scriptural that a man will not do well leading the church if he is unable to lead his own family. Read through the following Scriptures, noting what they have to say about the responsibilities of the husband/father in the home.

Genesis 2:24 _____

_____

Deuteronomy 6:4-9 _____

_____

Joshua 24:14-15 _____

_____

Job 1:1-5 _____

_____

Ephesians 5:21, 25-31 _____

_____

Colossians 3:12-21 _____

_____

1 Timothy 3:4-5 _____

_____

1 Peter 3:7 _____

_____

These Scriptures reveal that the man, as the spiritual head of his home, is commanded to minister to his family in four areas; in godly love, in teaching the truth of God, in discipline, and in being a priest to his family.

I. A MINISTRY OF LOVE

Ephesians 5:25 declares, "Husbands love your wives." Luke 15:11-24, in giving the story of the prodigal son, states that the prodigal's father "saw him coming, and was filled with loving pity and ran and embraced him and kissed him" (LB). Love is far more than an emotion. It is a choice of the will to seek the best for the other person. According to Ephesians 5, a husband is to love his wife as Christ loved the church. How did Christ love the church? Read Ephesians 5:25-27 again along with John 15:12-17 and Philippians 2:3-8, noting three characteristics of the love of Jesus Christ.

1. _____

2. _____

3. _____

One of the ways that the father/husband can demonstrate love is through praising and encouraging his family (positive reinforcement). The man who seeks opportunities to give such affirmation to his family will discover that much of the negativism, discouragement, and frustration that often exists in the home will be greatly diminished. And furthermore, many positive attitudes and actions will begin to emerge. As a *personal assignment* this week, keep a written record of the times you actually give praise and encouragement to your family. This could be enlightening.

II. A MINISTRY OF TEACHING

God's Word is clear that parents, especially fathers, have a responsibility for the spiritual education of their children. The church (and Christian schools) can be valuable contributors in their training, but this responsibility cannot be delegated to either the church or the school. A father, regardless of his educational background or occupation, must be an educator of his children. In the Deuteronomy 6 passage, did you notice the basic pattern for teaching/training children? Parents are to teach them in both formal and informal times. They are to talk to their children as they go through the regular activities of life. The implication of this passage is that parents spend enough time with their children so that they can seize opportunities to teach their children when those opportunities come along. There will be many informal times during a week to give instruction. (Note: This does not mean giving them hourly sermons.) There also needs to be time set aside for more formal instruction in the Word. In today's fast-paced society this will challenge the creativity of the father.

Take a few minutes, and write down some ideas about the formal training of your children. Write down some of the things that you have done or that you have heard that others have done, and prepare to share them in the group study.

_____

_____

_____

III. A MINISTRY OF DISCIPLINE

As one shows love to his children, and as he attempts to train them to be spiritually mature adults, he must exercise discipline. Basically the word *discipline* means "to train." The purpose of discipline is not to punish, but to train, guide, and teach. Within the word discipline is the root word "disciple." A man's children are his disciples and must be disciplined by him.

Discipline in the home includes several concepts. First, it is necessary to set rules and regulations that provide boundaries for appropriate behavior. These rules must be clear and understandable as well. A critical distinction must be made by the father between rebellion and childishness. The challenging of parental authority (rebellion) is to receive the rod of chastisement (Prov. 22:15; 29:15), but the rod is never to be used when the issue is immaturity or childishness. When the rules are willfully broken (after being understood), then the rod is to be applied. Please note that rules and regulations will change as the children grow and mature. What is appropriate for a two-year-old may not be appropriate for a twelve-year-old. Another concept in discipline is that a father is not to exasperate his children (Eph. 6:4). "Exasperate" means to frustrate, anger, embitter, or discourage. Improper discipline will exasperate a child. One author lists several ways that this can happen. A father exasperates his child when:

He abuses them physically.

He abuses them psychologically.

He neglects them.

He doesn't understand them.

He expects too much from them.

He puts them on a performance standard.

He forces them to accept his goals and ideas.

He won't admit his mistakes.[1]

A third concept relates to the goal of discipline. Ephesians 6:4 says, "Bring them up in the training and instruction of the Lord." The goal in discipline is to develop spiritually mature adults. It is important always to keep the finished product in mind.

IV. A MINISTRY OF PRAYER

All believers are priests according to 1 Peter 2:9. However, in a special sense, the husband/father has a unique priestly role in relationship to his family. A father represents God to his family through his love, teaching, and discipline. He represents his family to God through prayer. Prayer for his family is one of his greatest ministries and, yet, often one that is neglected. As our families are increasingly affected by the moral and spiritual darkness around us, fathers need to pray as Jesus did for His disciples that God would "keep them from the evil one" (John 17:15).

1. Gene Getz, *The Measure of a Family* (Glendale: Regal, 1976), pp. 85-89.

THE INNER LIFE OF CHURCH LEADERS

SESSION 4:
TIME AND PRIORITIES

The Bible is clear that we are stewards. A steward is one who has been given authority and responsibility over the resources and affairs of another. God has entrusted us with many things, such as creation, possessions, time, talent, spiritual gifts, families, and positions of ministry. A steward owns nothing himself but rather should manage faithfully those possessions or positions entrusted to his care. As stewards, we must recognize that all we have comes from God.

> Let a man so consider us, as servants of Christ and stewards of the mysteries of God. Moreover it is required in stewards that a man be found faithful (1 Cor. 4:1-2, NKJV).

> Timothy, guard what has been entrusted to your care (1 Tim. 6:20*a*).

> Each one should use whatever gift he has received to serve others, faithfully administering God's grace in its various forms (1 Pet. 4:10).

As spiritual leaders, elders and deacons have a greater accountability before God for the resources and responsibilities He has given them (James 3:1). As we study three areas of our stewardship responsibility, we need to remind ourselves that time, money, and spiritual gifts have been given to us on loan from God.

PREPARATORY ASSIGNMENTS:

1. Time is one of those valuable commodities that has been entrusted to us. Each of us is given days that contain twenty-four hours, and what we do with that time is important. We don't want to waste it but rather use it in the best possible ways. Read the following Scriptures, and note the truths about time that they contain.

   Psalm 90:10-12 _____

   _____

   Ecclesiastes 3:1, 17 _____

   _____

   Ephesians 5:15-16 _____

   _____

   John 4:34; 9:4; 17:4 _____

   _____

   James 4:13-15 _____

   _____

2. Read chapter 12 in *Spiritual Leadership* and pages 64-85 in *Ordering Your Private World*, and answer the following questions.

What is the greatest problem that we have with time? _____

_____

What can we learn from Jesus' use of time? _____

_____

How can we get more time for the things we think are important? _____

_____

What are the symptoms (if any) of disorganization in your life? _____

_____

According to Gordon MacDonald, if you do not budget your time, what will happen to it? _____

Do you think Sanders is correct when he says that the statement "I don't have the time" is the refuge taken by the small-minded and ineffectual person?

_____

_____

I. TIME MANAGEMENT

Dozens of books on time management are available, coming from the background of home, business, and Christian organizations. It would be impossible to discuss all the various tips and helps offered for time management. However, elders and deacons must deal with two basic concepts when attempting to be faithful stewards of time. These concepts are a biblical view of priorities and a proper view of budgeting time.

A. ESTABLISHING PRIORITIES

Almost everyone has experienced the frustration that comes with trying to handle the pressures and demands of life. How do we handle the key areas of our relationship with the Lord, our families, our work, and time for ourselves? J. Grant Howard, in his book *Balancing Life's Demands,* has some helpful ideas based on Matthew 22:34-40. Howard comments on Jesus' declaration that we are to love the Lord completely, and we are to love our neighbors as ourselves. Both commands are said to be of greater importance than all others. Furthermore, they are never mutually exclusive. We must love God and our neighbor at the same time. A third priority factor is not stated as an additional commandment, but it is suggested by the second. Therefore, we are looking at three top priorities; loving God, loving neighbors, and loving self. We must balance these responsibilities. Along with Howard's book, a work by Mark Littleton, *Escaping the Time Crunch*, is helpful, particularly pages 87-132, which deal with goals, priorities, and balanced living.

The concept given above does not eliminate the need to apply proved time management ideas. These ideas take on new meaning, however, when in the setting of divinely established priorities.

B. BUDGETING TIME

One begins a time budget as he would a financial budget. List your fixed time expenditures, such as employment and other established commitments that you have little or no control over (such as time spent in commuting). Other items such as time for sleeping, eating, and household chores are factored in.

In order to budget time effectively, we must have clear short-term and long-term goals. It is impossible to make good decisions about time if we have no clear idea regarding what we are trying to do. Written goals are extremely important for the leader. It is important to observe in the life of Christ that Jesus did have His goals and priorities clearly set, with the result that where, when, how, and to whom He would minister was clear to Him. He accomplished God's complete will without living at a frenzied pace. Good time management principles are reflected in Christ's life and ministry. For example, He knew how to say no to requests that did not fit into the will of God for him.

In using time wisely, we must develop a system for tracking our daily schedules. There is probably not a successful time manager alive who does not have a "to do" list that is used daily. On such a list, activities are noted and then prioritized. The "to do" list is used to guide the activities of the day.

For more helpful suggestions on time management, see *How to Get Control of Your Time and Your Life,* by Alan Lakein.

II. SABBATH PRINCIPLE

One area often neglected is the matter of sabbath rest. The word *sabbath* carries the idea of "ceasing" or "desisting." It speaks of a cessation from activity. Many leaders, like others around them, seem to be living in a state of constant fatigue. Exhaustion seems to be the norm for this perpetually tired generation. This situation needs to be seriously addressed. A burned out person is not a good leader. God's answer to this and to excellent time management is to build "sabbath" into our lives. Note the truths given in the following Scriptures.

Genesis 2:1-3 _____

_____

Exodus 20:9-11 _____

_____

Exodus 23:11-12 _____

_____

Exodus 31:12-17 _____

_____

Mark 3:1-4 _____

_____

Mark 2:27 _____

_____

Note the following passages, which reveal how Jesus "rested" during His very busy ministry: Matthew 15:21, 29; Mark 6:31, 46; 7:24; 9:30; Luke 4:42; 5:16; 9:10, 18; John 7:8-9.

From these verses a number of important truths emerge about the sabbath, truths that will help keep an individual from the condition commonly referred to as "burnout."

First, the sabbath *day* was given to the nation of Israel as a part of their over-all way of life. When the Mosaic law code was set aside as a rule of life, the sabbath *day* was no longer legislated.

Second, the sabbath *principle* was established at creation by God Himself. He established the work-rest cycle for the welfare of mankind.

Third, the sabbath *principle* is necessary today for physical, emotional, spiritual, and social well being. To violate the *principle* is to invite a condition of exhaustion that is brought on by continued damaging stress.

A QUESTION TO CONSIDER: Read pages 172-74 in *Ordering Your Private World.* Do you have a place of programmed rest in your week? _____

When we plan our lives and manage our time, then we can program in the needed sabbath principle and thus improve the quality of life, ministry, and leadership.

III. PERSONAL GOALS

Thomas Stevenin states that in order to achieve personal excellence, a leader needs to set goals in six vital areas (seminar notes on "How to Achieve Personal Excellence").

A. HEALTH AND PHYSICAL GOALS

Physical check up
Nutrition
Exercise
Relaxation
Stress management

B. HOME AND FAMILY GOALS

Time allocation
House and yard
Time with children
Time with spouse
Recreation time (24 hours per week)
Activities
New friends

C. PROFESSIONAL AND CAREER GOALS

Current job situation
Future position desired
Additional training needed
Habits that hold me back

D. FINANCIAL AND STEWARDSHIP GOALS

Current income/desired income
Long-term investments
Savings
Giving

E. TRAINING AND MENTAL GOALS

Courses
Books to read
Tapes to listen to
Mentors/groups/role models

F. SPIRITUAL AND EVANGELISTIC GOALS

Prayer and study time
New ministry area
Personal ministry to other person(s)
Fellowship/enrichment

A QUESTION TO CONSIDER: How do these goals affect my own life? Take twenty minutes or so and come up with two measurable and realistic goals in each of the six areas.

_____

_____

_____

_____

_____

_____

_____

_____

_____

SESSION 5:
GIFTS AND SERVICE

As faithful stewards, we must recognize and use the spiritual gifts given to us. The New Testament reveals that the proper employment of spiritual gifts is vital to the spiritual well-being of the church.

PREPARATORY ASSIGNMENT:

In preparation for this study area, read 1 Corinthians 12:7-11 and Ephesians 4:7-14, and answer the following questions.

What statements reveal that spiritual gifts are not for personal edification but are to benefit the whole church body? _____

_____

_____

Why are spiritual gifts given to believers? _____

_____

_____

Who determines what gift(s) each believer receives? _____

_____

When spiritual gifts are being used by believers in the church, what will be true of that church? What will not be true in that church? _____

_____

_____

_____

I. THE GENERAL MEANING OF SPIRITUAL GIFTS

It is important to define and describe spiritual gifts. The theological concept of spiritual gifts comes from several Greek words but primarily *charisma,* meaning "an endowment of God's grace, something given out of grace and not of debt; a spiritual working of God."[1] A spiritual gift, therefore, is imparted because of the grace of God. We might then define a spiritual gift as an ability given to an individual believer by God in order that the believer might serve God effectively in some particular way. It is part of our anointing by the Holy Spirit, who sets us apart as believer priests. We now have, therefore, both the position and the ability to serve the Lord effectively.

1. Stanton Richardson, *Studies in Biblical Theology* (St. Paul: St. Paul Bible College, 1969), 3:121.

When we investigate the Scripture passages on spiritual gifts, the following facts become clear. These facts include some assumptions about the gifts of the Spirit that deserve discussion that unfortunately cannot be included here.

Each believer has a spiritual gift, and possibly more than one.

Spiritual gifts are received at the moment of one's conversion and most likely are to be associated with the anointing ministry of the Spirit.

The gifts are given for ministry and edification within the Body of Christ, which strongly suggests that the local church is the primary place where gifts are used.

Although all gifts are needed in the church, some are more important than others.

Some gifts were permanently given, whereas others apparently were temporary, being important for the beginning years of the church.[2]

The believer controls the use of his gift and is, therefore, the one responsible for its use or non-use.

Like natural abilities, spiritual gifts can be developed and matured.

Spiritual gifts can be used with wrong motives, without love for others. They should not, of course, be used in this way, but sometimes this does take place.

Spiritual gifts are not the same as natural abilities or the same as the fruit of the Spirit.

Spiritual gifts are not abilities to work with some particular age group or in some particular place of service.

The first step in recognizing one's own gift(s) is to understand the gifts themselves. At this point a great deal of disagreement occurs on the actual number of spiritual gifts found in the New Testament and on the definitions for several of them. The three primary passages, Ephesians 4, Romans 12, and 1 Corinthians 12, give differing and overlapping lists.

II. THE PERMANENT KIND OF SPIRITUAL GIFTS

Eleven gifts were given at the beginning of the church age and continue on to the end of the church age. They are necessary for the ongoing spiritual health of the church.

---

2. A great deal of discussion persists among evangelicals regarding the permanent/temporary nature of spiritual gifts. For instance, the authors of this workbook have differing viewpoints. The division of the gifts into permanent and temporary categories as given in the main text is the view of Paul Benware, whereas Brian Harris believes that all the gifts given by God at Pentecost are still operational today. However, Harris makes three important distinctions. First, not all spiritual gifts are operational at all times or in all local churches. Second, some gifts, such as tongues, are of lesser importance (1 Cor. 12-14). And third, some gifts have a primary New Testament definition and a secondary contemporary definition. This view is found, for the most part, in *Nineteen Gifts of the Spirit* (Wheaton: Victor, 1974), by Leslie Flynn.

A. PASTOR-TEACHER

The gift of pastor-teacher is the ability to shepherd the people of God. The gift seems to include a sensitivity to the needs of believers in the flock as well as the ability to meet those needs. Since "teacher" is most likely linked to "pastor," and since one of the main responsibilities of a shepherd was to feed his flock, one with this gift has the capacity to handle the Word of God effectively. It must be remembered that this is a spiritual gift, not a church office.

B. TEACHING

The gift of teaching is the ability to make clear the truth of the Scriptures through systematic instruction and to do it in such a way that people can understand the truth and see something of its application to life.

C. EVANGELISM

The gift of evangelism is the ability to share the gospel clearly and to see noticeable results in that numerous individuals come to Christ as Savior.

D. EXHORTATION

The gift of exhortation is the ability to encourage and admonish others in their walk with Christ. The gift seems to include the two elements of challenge and comfort. This gift probably includes a sensitivity to people's situations as well as a discerning spirit.

E. HELPS (MINISTERING)

The gift of helps is the ability to aid believers in need, especially in physical and material ways. Those having this gift with ease come alongside those who have needs.

F. MERCY

The gift of mercy is the ability to deal effectively and lovingly with those who are sick and afflicted. Evidence of this gift includes the presence of cheerfulness when engaged in this ministry area.

G. ADMINISTRATION (GOVERNMENT)

The gift of administration is the ability to give organizational and superintending leadership to the church.

H. FAITH

The gift of faith if the ability to believe God in such a way that God is free to choose to act in powerful ways. Faith is not irrational but is characterized by an utter dependence on the Lord and not on human resources.

I. GIVING

The gift of giving is the ability to donate generously, cheerfully, and eagerly to the Body of Christ out of one's own resources. It may include the ability to make money and may also include a discerning spirit to know where and when to give.

J. KNOWLEDGE

The gift of knowledge is the ability to understand truth, to have illumination and insight that is unusual. If this applies to the days before the completion of the canon of Scripture, then it was a revelational gift for that time only. If for today, it would be interpretive in function and would apply to those with a higher level of understanding of God's truths and might particularly apply to Christian scholars.

K. WISDOM

The gift of wisdom is the ability to practically apply the Word of God to life's situations.

III. THE TEMPORARY KIND OF SPIRITUAL GIFTS

These are four gifts that were given at the beginning of the church age but apparently became unnecessary after that initial period ended. Their function was foundational in nature and not needed after the church had been established and the written Word of God had been completely given.

A. APOSTLE

The gift of apostleship was the ability to establish the church of Christ by preaching the word and verifying that preached word through the working of miracles. Although the word "apostle" has a general sense of "one who is sent," its usage as a spiritual gift takes on a technical meaning. The apostles were part of the church's foundation (Eph. 2:20). Once the doctrinal foundation of the church was established and once churches were actually begun, there was no need for the continuation of this gift.[3]

B. PROPHET

The gift of prophecy was the ability to set forth the truth of God having been received directly from God. It was also a foundational gift (Eph. 2:20). The word *prophecy* can, in a general sense, mean simply to "proclaim" or "preach." But in its usage as a spiritual gift it also includes foretelling the future and the receiving of truth directly from God. Once the canon of Scripture was completed and there was no new revelation given, there was no need for the gift of prophecy.[4]

C. TONGUES

The gift of tongues was the ability to speak in a foreign language that was unknown to the speaker. The purpose of the gift was to be a sign of coming judgment

---

3. Some believe that this gift still exists today in a secondary sense, as one sent out as a cross-cultural missionary.
4. Some believe that this gift still exists today in a secondary sense in the "forth-telling" of the Word of God, that is, in preaching and teaching.

on unbelieving Israel. The interpretation of tongues was the ability to translate from one language into another, when one of those languages was unknown to the translator. Clearly these gifts were supernatural in character.

D. HEALINGS (MIRACLES)

The gift of healings was the ability to supernaturally and instantaneously bring healing to one afflicted with disease or deformity. The purpose of healings and miracles was to authenticate the new revelation from God. Although God can and does bring healing to people, and sometimes sovereignly suspends natural law, *these gifts are not possessed by people today.* Since the primary purpose of verifying the message is no longer needed, the gifts are not needed.

These definitions and descriptions are not the final and complete word on the subject of spiritual gifts, but they do give us a platform from which to discuss and evaluate the spiritual gifts that have been given to each of us.

Several proved steps aid in discovering one's spiritual gift. First, the leader must have a desire to know his gifts and to seek God's discernment in finding them. The apostle Paul wanted believers to discover the spiritual resources that were theirs, and he prayed for that. This is a legitimate subject for our praying as well. Second, he should seek the advice and counsel of godly believers. Many times someone who knows the individual can recognize a gift when the recipient cannot. Third, it is helpful to observe carefully the ministry experiences of the past. Those where there has been relative ease and where there have been good results probably indicate the areas where one's spiritual abilities lie. Fourth, various tests and questionnaires are available to help the leader find his gift.

Paul exhorted Timothy, "Make full proof of thy ministry" (2 Tim. 4:5, KJV), and "Stir up the gift of God, which is in thee" (2 Tim. 1:6, KJV). As faithful stewards, we must put much effort into the preparation and development of our spiritual gifts. Happy is the church whose leaders know and use them.

SOME QUESTIONS TO CONSIDER:

What do you believe is your spiritual gift(s)? _____

_____

Why do you think that this is your gift? _____

_____

_____

Ask a family member or a mature believer what he thinks is your spiritual gift. Why does he think so? _____

_____

_____

In what way do you believe your spiritual gift can best be used in the church? _____

_____

_____

_____

SESSION 6:
FINANCES AND ACCOUNTABILITY

Money talks. It says a great deal about us. It can reveal that we are stingy or that we are generous, wise or unwise, spiritually mature or immature, users of money or worshipers of it. An elder or deacon who is committed to obeying and serving God must be a faithful steward of his finances. It is essential that the leader have this area of life under the control of the Spirit of God and the Word of God.

PREPARATORY ASSIGNMENTS:

1. The Lord Jesus Christ taught often on the matter of money and material things. Please read the following Scripture portions, and write down your discoveries about money from Christ's teachings.

    Matthew 6:2-4 _____

    _____

    Matthew 6:19-21, 24 _____

    _____

    Matthew 16:26 _____

    _____

    Matthew 22:17-22 _____

    _____

    Matthew 25:14-30 _____

    _____

    Mark 12:41-44 _____

    _____

    Luke 12:22-34 _____

    _____

    Luke 16:10-14 _____

    _____

2. The apostle Paul also taught often on the issue of money and its use. What truths can you find in the following Scripture passages?

    Romans 12:13 _____

    _____

Romans 13:6-7 _____

_____

Philippians 4:10-19 _____

_____

1 Corinthians 16:1-2 _____

_____

1 Thessalonians 4:11-12; Titus 3:14 _____

_____

1 Timothy 3:3, 8 _____

_____

1 Timothy 6:6-11 _____

_____

1 Timothy 6:17 _____

_____

Galatians 6:6-10 _____

_____

I. PRINCIPLES OF MONEY MANAGEMENT

Given below are some biblical principles of money management noted by Ron Blue in his book *Master Your Money*. He drew these four helpful principles from the parable of the talents in Matthew 25:14-30.[1]

A. GOD OWNS EVERYTHING

The basis of study on stewardship is found in one definition of steward: a steward is one who owns nothing. This must be restated in our study on finances. We must be convinced that all we have, all we earn, and all we have the potential to earn comes from God. This is a key issue, since it reveals our attitudes. Blue says this principle leads to three implications. First, "God has the right to whatever He wants when He wants it." The owner has the right to give but also to ask for its return. Second, "Not only is my giving decision a spiritual decision, but every spending decision is a spiritual decision." The owner has a say in how his property is used and demands accountability. And third, "You can't fake stewardship." Your checkbook is a record of your stewardship.

B. WE ARE IN A GROWTH PROCESS

God uses money and possessions to help us conform to His image. Money is "a tool, a test, and a testimony." Money is a great attention getter. God will use the

1. Ron Blue, *Master Your Money* (Nashville: Nelson, 1986), pp. 19-21.

38

money we have or do not have as a *tool* to get our attention. Once He has our attention, He can teach us what He wants us to learn. Money is also a *test*. Our handling of money and possessions tests our faithfulness, commitment, and spirituality. How we handle our money is a *testimony*. Christians are to be different from the world. We must be biblical in our attitudes towards money and in our giving, spending, and saving habits.

C. THE AMOUNT IS NOT IMPORTANT

In the parable of the talents, both the slave entrusted with five talents and the slave entrusted with two talents received equal commendations. The amount of financial resources is not important, but what we do with what we have is important.

D. FAITH REQUIRES ACTION

In the parable of the talents, the wicked servant is condemned for failing to take action with his talent. God holds us accountable for what we do or don't do with our finances. We are between the proverbial rock and a hard place. Therefore, let us use our finances as God would have us to.

A crucial area is that of giving. Obviously God does not need our money. Yet He is interested in how and why we give. In 2 Corinthians 8 and 9, the apostle Paul gives a number of important principles for giving. Please read through these two chapters, and write down five of those principles.

1. _____
2. _____
3. _____
4. _____
5. _____

II. PLANNING FOR MONEY MANAGEMENT

A final matter needs to be considered, and that is the issue of a budget. A family budget is a spiritual document. It reveals faith in God's provision, it expresses our priorities, and it shows our commitment to serving God.

A budget is simply a plan for using the financial resources God has given us. It can be as simple or complex as you wish. There are several excellent resources to help you get started if you do not have a budget. *Master Your Money,* by Ron Blue, *How to Succeed with Your Money,* by George M. Bowman, and numerous books by Larry Burkett (e.g., *How to Manage Your Money, Debt-Free Living*) can be of great practical help.

An elder or deacon who has money problems of his own making sets a poor example for the flock of God and undercuts his own ability to lead. A leader must be a responsible steward of all that God has entrusted to him, whether time, gifts, or money.

SESSION 7:
CONVICTIONS AND STANDARDS

Most would agree that the standards of our society are fast slipping away from those high standards of Scripture. This erosion has affected the local body of Christ. Activities and lifestyles that were once universally rejected as unacceptable Christian behavior are now engaged in freely by many believers. For example, what is viewed on television today in a rather casual and routine way would have deeply shocked thoughtful Christians twenty-five years ago and would have been categorically rejected as unacceptable. These changes have caused confusion among younger and older Christians alike. One who wishes to serve as an elder or deacon in the local church must deal with the issue of behavioral standards for himself, and his family, and the church.

I. TYPES OF PERSONAL STANDARDS

Leaders will be expected by the people they serve to have thought through the controversial issues of the day and to have convictions regarding these issues. Therefore leaders must understand how one arrives at personal standards. Normally the first response would be to turn to the Scriptures. However, this leads to a problem because some of the controversial issues of the day are not specifically referred to in the Bible. At this point, three terms need to be defined: *absolutes, convictions,* and *preferences.* Noting the differences between these words will help in the setting of personal standards and in applying them to those we lead.

A. ABSOLUTES

Absolutes are those standards or directives for faith, doctrine, or behavior that are set forth clearly in the Scriptures. For each absolute, there will always be a specific scriptural reference. The Ten Commandments are an excellent example from the Old Testament. The apostle Paul's command in 1 Thessalonians 4:3 to "avoid sexual immorality" is a New Testament example. Biblical absolutes are not subject to change. They are consistent from age to age and culture to culture. Absolutes touch areas of faith and practice. There are certain things a Christian must believe and do.

Take a few minutes and write down some absolutes in areas of both faith and practice.

_____

_____

_____

_____

B. CONVICTIONS

Convictions are personal standards that are based on biblical principles. However, they are not as clear-cut or rigid as absolutes. They are personal standards based upon one's understanding of biblical passages and truths. They may change with the passage of time. Absolutes never change, but convictions are more temporal and will vary. It is important for an elder or deacon to know what are biblical absolutes and what are personal convictions.

A leader needs to have strong personal convictions that are clearly supported by scriptural principles. But he must be aware of the reality that other believers may not arrive at the same convictions, even using the same portions of God's Word. While one must be willing to defend and die for the absolutes, the believer may want to leave room for negotiation and differences in the area of convictions. Sad to say, it is often in the realm of convictions that the church experiences some of its bloodiest internal battles.

Convictions are often controversial. A sample of a personal conviction might be the use of alcoholic beverages. The Bible clearly teaches that drunkenness is wrong (Eph. 5:18). However, it does not clearly require that believers should totally abstain. It may be that I choose not to drink any alcoholic beverages at any time. I might view alcohol as harmful to my body, and I am to honor God with my body (1 Cor. 6:20). It may be that I am convinced that my drinking would hurt other believers in their walk with Christ (1 Cor. 8:7-13). These together with other Scripture portions may lead me to the strong personal conviction of total abstinence. Another believer, however, may hold that moderate drinking is part of his Christian liberty. It must be remembered that convictions should be based on scriptural teachings or principles.

Read Romans 14, and come up with some guidelines for establishing personal convictions.

_____

_____

_____

C. PREFERENCES

Preferences are simply a matter of personal taste or selection. They do not have scriptural basis but simply reflect the likes and the dislikes of the individual. Preferences usually have to do with behavior and practice rather than belief. Examples of preference occur in the areas of clothing styles, musical likes and dislikes, forms of worship, leisure-time activities, and other similar matters.

II. ATTITUDES ON PERSONAL STANDARDS

When discussing the issue of personal standards, two terms usually arise: legalism and license. As one studies church history, it becomes apparent that Christians have struggled to maintain a balance between these two extremes. Those inclined to _license_ must realize that the freedom they have in Christ does not give them a free rein. Yes, Christ has set us free; however this is not freedom to indulge our sinful natures but freedom to love and serve Christ and His people (see Rom. 6:1-14; 1 Cor. 11:23—12:1; Gal. 5:13).

On the other hand, those inclined to *legalism,* who define spirituality by a list of do's and don'ts, must heed the words of Paul in Galatians 5:1: "It is for freedom that Christ has set us free. Stand firm then, and do not let yourselves be burdened again by a yoke of slavery." The believer is not to live by law codes but by the Spirit within him (Rom. 8:5-11; Gal. 5:16-18).

To be balanced we must live our lives and make our choices with a view to glorifying God through a life of loving obedience and restraint. We need to look carefully at the Word of God for direction and be careful how our living affects other believers. Since leaders do exert great influence, they must especially be wise and alert in this area of life.

CONCLUDING ASSIGNMENT:

As you read through the following list, designate whether an item is an absolute, a personal conviction, or a preference. Prepare to discuss your conclusions, noting scriptural references for absolutes and convictions.

ISSUE	BIBLICAL ABSOLUTE	PERSONAL CONVICTION	PREFERENCE
Faithful attendance of church services			
Anti-abortion stand			
Commitment to prayer			
Opposition to pornography			
Refusal to watch television			
Singing of old hymns of the faith			
Men with stylish haircuts			
Women wearing stylish clothes			
Attending all church services			
Going to professional sporting events on Sunday			
Dressing modestly			
Worshiping on *Sunday* morning			
Dancing			
Smoking			
Listening to Christian rock music			
Attending the theater or movies			
Listening to contemporary Christian music			
Allowing your children to go "trick or treating" on Halloween			
Driving a luxury car			
Profit-making sales in the church			
Gambling (playing the lottery)			
Homosexuality			
Drums in the worship service			
Drinking alcoholic beverages			

STUDY AREA 2
The Biblical Ideals for Church Leaders

At the heart of good leadership is character. Excellence in leadership and excellence of character are inseparably linked. A person with management skills but lacking in personal integrity will inevitably be a force for destruction in the local church. Leaders are needed badly, but not just any kind of leader. Robert Murray McCheyne once stated, "My people's greatest need is my personal holiness." It comes as no surprise then that there is a strong emphasis in the Scriptures on the godly character of those who would lead the church of Jesus Christ.

It is important and appropriate that time is devoted to a study of the character qualities of leaders found in 1 Timothy 3 and Titus 1. Three sessions will be spent in the investigation of these twenty character qualities. The list given in this study combines the Titus and Timothy passages and combines the biblical qualifications for elder and deacon, making it a list of "leadership" qualifications. (Note that the primary differences between an elder and a deacon would be that an elder must be "apt to teach" and that he should reflect a greater spiritual maturity, which would include having greater "life experience.")

TEXT FOR THIS STUDY AREA:

Gene A. Getz. *The Measure of a Man.* Ventura, Calif.: Regal, 1985.

THE BIBLICAL IDEALS FOR CHURCH LEADERS
SESSION 1:
QUALIFICATIONS AND EXPLANATIONS (A)

PREPARATORY ASSIGNMENTS:

In preparing for this session: (1) read Titus 1:5-9 and 1 Timothy 3:1-13; (2) read chapters 1-5 in *The Measure of a Man*; (3) fill in the "Definition/Description" of qualities A-D, after reading these study notes and Getz's discussion; and (4) fill in the "Identification/Application" for qualities 1-4. In this part you are trying to answer the question, "If a man was characterized by this quality, how would it be seen in the man's life today?"

I. SOME PRELIMINARY OBSERVATIONS ON LEADERSHIP QUALIFICATIONS

Before looking at the individual qualifications given in Timothy and Titus, it is important to make several general observations.

A. THE NEED FOR A BALANCED BUT SERIOUS VIEW

The biblical list presents God's ideal leader. This is the kind of person God wants to lead His people. No person will ever perfectly fulfill this list of qualities, but this does not mean that the standard can be set aside as an impossibility. It must be maintained in leadership evaluation. It must not be set aside either in theory or in practice.

A QUESTION TO CONSIDER: What results in a church when the biblical list is not consciously followed in leadership selection? _____

_____

B. THE EMPHASIS IS TO BE ON THE PRESENT

The Titus and Timothy passages focus on the present life of the man and not on his past ("A man must be . . ."). If a man's past were the issue, no one would qualify. An individual's past sins and failures or his past spiritual successes or reputation are not the issue. The issue is his present spiritual maturity.

A QUESTION TO CONSIDER: What are some dangers in dwelling on a man's past and not on his present spiritual situation? _____

_____

C. THERE IS AN EQUALITY IN IMPORTANCE

Churches will sometimes focus on a couple of the qualifications and neglect the others. To do this is to raise those few to the level of primary importance. But all are equally important. The apostle Paul does not mark out any quality as of primary importance. (This would be true even if the first one, "above reproach," is viewed as a general statement of qualification that encompasses all the rest.)

A QUESTION TO CONSIDER: What happens when a church focuses on just a few of the qualifications and neglects the others?

II. THE BIBLICAL LIST OF LEADERSHIP QUALIFICATIONS (1)

A. ABOVE REPROACH

1 Timothy 3:2 declares: "Now the overseer must be above reproach. . . ." A companion statement is found in 3:7, which says "he must have a good reputation with outsiders." In the letter to Titus, Paul uses the word "blameless" several times (Titus 1:6-7).

Some believe that these are thesis statements, overarching statements that introduce and summarize all of Paul's qualifications for leaders. This may be the case. On the other hand, they are probably synonymous expressions that together constitute one qualification among many.

"Blameless" comes from the Greek adjective *anenkletos,* which "signifies that which cannot be called to account, i.e., with nothing laid to one's charge (as the result of public investigation). It implies not merely acquittal but the absence of even a charge or accusation against a person."[1]

"Reproach" comes from a similar Greek word, *anepileptos,* meaning literally "that cannot be laid hold of, hence, not open to censure, irreproachable."[2] These are sobering terms. They seem to be grading men on a pass/fail system with no room in the middle. Either a man is above reproach or he is not. A key point here is that it is others who judge us. The emphasis is not on judgment of ourselves. It is a fact of life that even when an outsider examines our lives and finds them blameless, we always know that we could have done better. If we were to judge ourselves carefully, we would always find some area of inadequacy. Paul is telling Timothy and Titus to look for leaders who stand up to rigid investigation and examination. There is, of course, a necessary place for personal evaluation. However, in this instance Paul is speaking of an outside investigation.

B. THE HUSBAND OF ONE WIFE

This is probably the most controversial of the qualifications. Some have said this statement declares that a divorced man cannot serve as an elder or deacon. Others have stated that this is a requirement that an elder be married. Still others

1. W. E. Vine, *Expository Dictionary of New Testament Words* (Westwood, N.J.: Revell, 1962), 1:131.
2. Ibid.

have viewed this as a prohibition of polygamy. And there have been a number of other interpretations.

Probably the simplest interpretation of this passage is that the apostle Paul is referring to a man's character, that is, that a leader must be "a one-woman man." The great issue here is moral purity. Paul is stating that it is God's will that sexual expression and involvement be restricted to one's own wife. Sex is a beautiful gift of God and, if one is single, is to be reserved exclusively for one's future wife; if married, then for one's present wife.

The character of the man is emphasized here, not just that he has one wife. A man who has a wife but secretly desires another woman would certainly not be fulfilling this qualification.

C. TEMPERATE

The Greek word *nephalios* speaks of one who is self-controlled and not guided by passion. He is one who is sober, calm, and balanced in his life.

D. PRUDENT

The word *prudent* describes one who is serious and earnest about spiritual matters. This does not mean that he is melancholy or humorless but that in regard to the sacred things he is serious minded.

(BIBLICAL LIST OF LEADERSHIP QUALIFICATIONS continues on pp. 50 and 53.)

QUALITY	DEFINITION/DESCRIPTION	IDENTIFICATION/APPLICATION
Blameless		
Husband of One Wife		
Temperate		
Prudent		

THE BIBLICAL IDEALS FOR CHURCH LEADERS
SESSION 2:
QUALIFICATIONS AND EXPLANATIONS (B)

PREPARATORY ASSIGNMENT:

In preparation for this session: (1) read chapters 6-13 in *The Measure of a Man,* and (2) fill in the "Definition/Description" and "Identification/Application" for qualities E-L.

THE BIBLICAL LIST OF LEADERSHIP QUALIFICATIONS (2) (Continued from Session 1)

E. GOOD BEHAVIOR

The Greek word *kosmios* emphasizes the idea of an orderly, modest, and respectable lifestyle.[1] He is one who would reject the extremes of legalism and license and lives his life decently and in order.

F. GIVEN TO HOSPITALITY

The leader is to be one who is fond of using his home and resources to benefit others. The leader's possessions are to be used to help others. There is not only an *act* involved but an *attitude* of generosity as well.

G. APT TO TEACH

The Greek word *didaktikos* means "skilled in teaching," which is closely related to *didaktos,* meaning "primarily what can be taught."[2] The sense of this adjective is that a man is teachable and is then able to teach others. This does not require that a man must have the gift of teaching. The actual teaching may be one-on-one or in a class of hundreds. An elder must know and understand the Word of God and then be able to pass on that understanding. The context implies that his teaching is not to be argumentative or quarrelsome but instructive and corrective.

H. NOT GIVEN TO WINE

Ephesians 5:18 commands the believer: "Do not get drunk with wine which leads to debauchery, instead, be filled with the Spirit." The key concept in Ephesians 5, 1 Timothy 3, and Titus 1 is the same. Mature believers are to be controlled by the Holy Spirit and by nothing else. A leader is not to be controlled by wine. Although this directive is not an absolute prohibition against wine, it probably is wisest, in our indulgent culture, to take the position of total abstinence.

---

1. A. T. Robertson, *Word Pictures in the New Testament* (Nashville: Broadman, 1931), 4:572.
2. W. E. Vine, *Expository Dictionary of New Testament Words* (Westwood, N.J.: Revell, 1962), 4:111-12.

I. NOT SELF-WILLED

This looks at that quality of pleasing others rather than self. The Greek *authades* is an old word meaning self-pleasing or arrogant.[3] The leader cannot be one who demands his own way or lives by his own authority.

J. NOT QUICK TEMPERED

The focus of this word is on the idea of being suddenly upset (*orgilos*). A leader must not have a "short fuse" or be one who flares up easily and quickly.

K. NOT PUGNACIOUS

The Greek word *amachos* literally means "not a fighter."[4] The leader is not to be one who is involved in physical violence. He must be able to control his spirit.

L. UNCONTENTIOUS

A contentious person destroys the unity of the church because he is combative. He is quarrelsome, readily using emotional violence on others. He characteristically struggles against others.

(BIBLICAL LIST OF LEADERSHIP QUALIFICATIONS continues on p. 53.)

3. Robertson, *Word Pictures*, 4:599.
4. Vine, *Expository Dictionary*, 2:146.

QUALITY	DEFINITION/DESCRIPTION	IDENTIFICATION/APPLICATION
Good Behavior		
Given to Hospitality		
Apt to Teach		
Not Given to Wine		
Not Self-willed		
Not Quick Tempered		
Not Pugnacious		
Uncontentious		

SESSION 3:
QUALIFICATIONS AND EXPLANATIONS (C)

PREPARATORY ASSIGNMENTS:

In preparation for this session: (1) read chapters 14-21 in *The Measure of a Man*, and (2) fill in the "Definition/Description" and "Identification/Application" for qualities M-T.

THE BIBLICAL LIST OF LEADERSHIP QUALIFICATIONS (3) (Continued from Session 2)

M. GENTLE

The Greek word *epieikes* has the idea of that which is "seemly, fitting; hence equitable, fair, moderate, forbearing, not insisting on the letter of the law; it expresses that considerateness that looks humanely and reasonably at the facts of a case . . . (it is in association with meekness in James 3:17, as a quality of wisdom from above)."[1] This quality is the opposite of being quick tempered and contentious.

N. FREE FROM THE LOVE OF MONEY

Money must never be the priority of the leader. Although others may use money for status, power, or security, the leader must not. Money, of course, is not in itself evil. In fact, it is one of God's gifts to us, given to be used for His glory. Money and the things money can buy can become a problem when they come between the believer and God. Money is a tool for doing God's will. It is a means to an end, not an end in itself.

O. MANAGES HIS OWN HOUSE WELL

He is to have the love of his wife and the respect of his children. There is to be no rebelliousness in the family. The children are to be professing believers. He does not act as as harsh dictator but as a loving leader in his home. The home is certainly a key area in discovering the true character of a leader or potential leader.

P. GOOD REPUTATION

Those who are outside the church view the man favorably. They may not agree with his religious convictions, but nevertheless they see his life as free from wrongdoing and characterized by doing good. The biblical prophet Daniel is an excellent example of this quality.

---

1. W. E. Vine, *Expository Dictionary of New Testament Words* (Westwood, N.J.: Revell, 1962), 2:145.

Q. LOVES WHAT IS GOOD

His desire is for those things that are morally honorable and pleasing to God. This quality goes beyond just doing good to the level of desiring that which is good. This man stays as far away from sin as possible.

R. JUST

The Greek word *dikaios* denotes a state of being right, or right conduct.[2] For a leader particularly the word can carry with it the idea of being wise, fair, and discerning in his dealings with issues and with others. He is just, or righteous, in those dealings.

S. HOLY

A holy, or devout, person is one who has made a decision to turn from sin to God and then lives out the ramifications of that decision in his daily lifestyle. The emphasis of this quality is on one's behavior and attitude toward sin.

T. NOT A NOVICE

The Greek word *neophutos* was used of a newly planted tree, which lacked the root system to ensure stability. The basic concept is that the leader (especially the elder) must be one who has had a sufficient amount of time (years) to mature in the Lord. He has had life experience. He has been challenged, tested, even tempted, and found to be above reproach. This qualification is given to keep the new believer from temptation, from thinking he has attained spiritual maturity when he has not. The Jews commonly viewed the age of thirty as the minimum age for one to be an elder in the community. Although the Bible does not give such an age restriction, the term "elder" does reflect years as well as spiritual maturity.

PERSONAL PROJECT: On pages 215-18 of *The Measure of a Man* you will find some questions and an evaluation scale to help you rate yourself in relationship to the qualities you have been studying. After circling the appropriate number on each question, note the two lowest and set up a priority list for personal action in order to address those areas.

---

2. Ibid., 2:283.

QUALITY	DEFINITION/DESCRIPTION	IDENTIFICATION/APPLICATION
Gentle		
Free from the Love of Money		
Manages His Own House Well		
Good Reputation		
Loves What Is Good		
Just		
Holy		
Not a Novice		

SESSION 4:
SERVANTHOOD AND AUTHORITY

At the beginning of this manual certain basic assumptions were given. One of these was that biblical leadership is a position of servanthood rather than lordship. This communicates the idea that spiritual leaders must model the concept of the servant-leader, a concept that is found in a number of places in the New Testament. However, as the leader grapples with this concept, he is faced with two apparently contrasting ideas. As a result, he often finds himself vacillating from one extreme to the other in his attempt to be a servant-leader. And this is understandable when we reflect on the contrasts that apparently exist between being a servant and being a leader.

A Servant	*A Leader*
Follows direction	Gives directions
Is accountable to others	Holds others accountable
Looks to others for evaluation	Evaluates others
Has little or no authority	Has much authority

Another problem found in functioning as a servant-leader is the traditional form of appointment of leaders in most evangelical churches. Usually the congregation elects the leaders through consensus. Because the leaders are elected, congregations will often view their elders and deacons as their personal representatives (servants) to do their bidding and carry out their desires. Other congregations elect the elders but refuse to give them authority to lead or make decisions without congregational approval.

In 2 Corinthians 4:5, the apostle Paul states that he preached "Christ Jesus as Lord, and ourselves as your servants for Jesus' sake." There is one Lord who gives the orders and directions, and that is Jesus. Leaders are His servants. In a secondary sense they also function as servants of God's people. But it is to Jesus the Lord that leaders are ultimately accountable. Whereas there is (and must be) accountability on the human level, the leader's primary responsibility is to the Lord. The leader serves the people by meeting their needs, but he is not required to comply with every call or respond to every desire. He is like the shepherd who feeds, guards, and guides his flock but does not fulfill every whim of the sheep. One author has said, "If everyone in the church is your boss and you're the servant, you've got an absolutely intolerable position. Yes, you lead by serving, but the major expression of your service is your leadership. . . . If my gift is leading . . . then my serving is leading."[1]

1. Fred Smith, *Learning to Lead* (Waco, Tex.: Word, 1986), pp. 24-25.

PREPARATORY ASSIGNMENTS:

The idea of a servant-leader is a difficult idea for many to grasp and turn into a leadership approach. At this point: (1) read chapter 3 in *Spiritual Leadership*, by Oswald Sanders, and (2) read Mark 10:35-45, and respond to the following questions.

I. THE CONCEPT OF THE SERVANT-LEADER

A. BACKGROUND OF CHRIST'S TEACHING ON LEADERSHIP, MARK 10:35-41

1. *The Request of James and John, 10:35-27* (note Matt. 19:27; 20:20).

What was their request? _____

_____

_____

What do you think prompted their request? _____

_____

_____

2. *The Response of Jesus, 10:38-40.*

What was Christ's response? _____

_____

_____

Do you think Christ was rebuking them for their request? Why or why not?

_____

_____

_____

3. *The Response of James and John, 10:39.*

What did these two say? _____

_____

_____

What might their statement reveal about themselves? _____

_____

_____

4. *The Reaction of the Ten Disciples, 10:41.*

What was their reaction? _____

_____

_____

Why do you suppose these men reacted as they did? _____

_____

_____

B. SUBSTANCE OF CHRIST'S TEACHING ON LEADERSHIP, MARK 10:42-45

     1. *Leadership Authority That Comes by Position, 10:42.*

What generally characterizes this kind of authority? _____

_____

_____

Why does Jesus say, "You know," in verse 42? _____

_____

_____

     2. *Leadership Authority That Comes by Serving, 10:43-45.*

How does one become a great Christian leader? _____

_____

_____

Is a desire to excel acceptable to Christ? _____

_____

_____

How does Christ exemplify the servant-leader role? _____

_____

_____

C. SUMMARIZING CHRIST'S TEACHING ON LEADERSHIP

     What do you consider to be the three key ideas taught by the Lord Jesus in this passage?

1. _____

2. _____

3. _____

SOME QUESTIONS TO CONSIDER:

Is an elder accountable to the congregation? Explain. _____

_____

_____

In your experience, when have you observed leadership authority most often being abused?

_____

II. THE AUTHORITY OF THE SERVANT-LEADER

The servant-leader derives his authority to lead from two sources.

The first source is the authority of his office. As a man is placed into the office of elder or deacon, whether by election or appointment, he assumes and is given authority because of having that position. Authority lies in the office itself, just as it does for the mayor, governor, or president. When a man enters the office he has authority, and when he departs the office he leaves the authority behind.

A second source of authority comes from the voluntary submission of those who are being led. This was Jesus' emphasis in Mark 10:35-45. A spiritual leader may assume the first source of authority but must cultivate the second source. It is possible, of course, for an individual to have this second kind of authority without holding an office.

The question naturally arises as to how the leader obtains this voluntary submission. This submission comes when it is evident that the elder or deacon meets the biblical qualifications for the office and is properly performing the functions of that office. Also, it must be clear to the ones being led that the leader is there to serve the people and not himself. When the congregation recognizes the spiritual qualifications of the leader and senses his servant spirit, they are far more willing to submit to leadership. This second source of leadership authority is crucial. Without it elders and deacons will never be able to effectively lead the church.

A QUESTION TO CONSIDER:

What could be expected of leadership where there is leadership authority by position only? _____

_____

_____

Leaders must lead. And, if they are going to lead, they must possess and exercise authority. The difference between biblical leadership and secular leadership is not that biblical leadership is characterized by a lack of authority. It differs from secular leadership in its motivation and purpose. An individual receives biblical authority from being a genuine servant and from occupying a position that has God-given authority. A servant-leader, then, is one who has voluntarily placed himself under the authority of the Lord Jesus Christ in order to work out His will by serving others while in a place of leadership.

There are countless examples of Bible characters who were given authority by God (e.g., Luke 6:12-13; Matt. 28:18-20; 2 Cor. 12:12; Eph. 6:1-4; Ex. 20:12; Num. 12, 16, 17).

A. THE PURPOSES OF GOD-GIVEN LEADERSHIP AUTHORITY

Read the following Scriptures, observing three purposes for authority:
2 Corinthians 4:1-6; 10:8; 13:2, 10; Ephesians 4:11-12; 1 Peter 5:1-5; 1 Thessalonians 5:14; Acts 20:28-30; Galatians 6:1.

1. _____

2. _____

3. _____

B. THE RESPONSE TO GOD-GIVEN LEADERSHIP AUTHORITY

   The Scriptures also have instructions to those who are under leadership authority. Note the three responses mentioned in the following Scriptures: 1 Thessalonians 5:12-13; Hebrews 13:17; 1 Corinthians 16:16; 1 Timothy 5:17-18.

1. _____

2. _____

3. _____

SESSION 5:
ORGANIZATION AND ACTION

I. THE NECESSITY OF CHURCH ORGANIZATION

Down through the centuries certain individuals have attacked the ideas that the local church is to be organized, believing instead that organization hinders the free working of the Holy Spirit. Their view is that the church should simply get together for informal times of Bible study, prayer, and worship. It is believed that the early church was not organized and thus operated in the freedom and power of the Holy Spirit. However, though the early church did operate in the enabling power of the Spirit, there are numerous evidences of organization in the New Testament local church. What are some of these?

Acts 20:7; 1 Corinthians 14:40; 16:1-2; Hebrews 10:25 _____

_____

Acts 14:23; 20:17-30; Philippians 1:1; Titus 1:5-7 _____

_____

1 Corinthians 5:1-13; 2 Thessalonians 3:6, 14 _____

_____

1 Timothy 5:9-10; Acts 2:47; 5:11-14; 6:1, 7 _____

_____

Acts 2:42-47 _____

_____

Romans 15:25-28; 1 Corinthians 16:1-2; 2 Corinthians 8:16-21 _____

_____

Those who attack the organization of the church will also make the accusation that organization hinders the working of the Holy Spirit. Those who hold such a view presuppose that the work of the Spirit is always spontaneous and functions best on the "spur of the moment." However, since the Holy Spirit is fully God, He knows all things from eternity past to eternity future. He can work in directing the setting up of organizational structures or in the more spontaneous outworking in the life of the Body.

Someone has said that management is not a substitute for anything spiritual but is rather a supplement. The question, "Is organization spiritual?" can be answered with a strong *yes*. It is understood, of course, that the organization of the church must take its directives from the teaching and example of the Word of God and be sensitive to the leading of the Spirit. The church needs to be organized and to do things "decently and in order" (1 Cor. 14:40, KJV).

II. The Leader in Church Organization

A primary responsibility of the leaders of the local church is to organize the work and give direction to the ministry. A good leader is not one who simply maintains the status quo but rather is one who sets the direction for the church. Many definitions could be given to leadership.

> Leadership is the discipline of deliberately exerting special influence within a group to move it toward goals of beneficial permanence that fulfill the group's real needs.[1]

> Leadership is influence, the ability of one person to influence others to and follow his or her lead.[2]

> The exercise of one's spiritual gifts under the call of God to serve a certain group of people in achieving the goals God has given them toward the end of glorifying Christ.[3]

These definitions, along with many similar ones, include three basic factors in good leadership. First, a leader knows where he is going. He has vision and goals in mind. Without this there is a great deal of motion without meaning. Second, a leader has the ability to persuade others to join him. He is able to communicate his vision to others and to motivate them. Third, a leader generally knows what is best for others. He is sensitive and wise. A good shepherd will usually know what is best for his sheep. He does not lead for his own pleasure or glory but for the edification of the people who follow him.

The leader, therefore, plays the critical role in setting goals for the church. Without this work of organizing the ministry of the church, the church will flounder and never fulfill God's purposes for it.

III. The Process of Church Organization

Since organization is biblical, and since leaders are to give vision and direction to the church, the next question to be answered is: "How does the spiritual leader begin to organize the work of the church?" There is much to do and many things to get done. Where does one start? The important responsibility of the deacons and elders is to take the initiative in leading the church in the reaching of their goals. There are three basic factors that in proper sequence constitute the process of healthy church organization.

A. Explanation of the Organizational Factors

1. *Mission.* The mission of any church or organization is its reason for existence. The mission statement answers the question, "Why do we exist?" The word "mission" emphasizes our unique purpose for existence. Does your church have a written mission statement? If "yes," what is it? If "no," what do you believe it should be?

---

1. John Haggai, *Lead On* (Waco, Tex.: Word, 1986), p.4.
2. Oswald Sanders, *Spiritual Leadership,* 3d ed., rev. (Chicago: Moody, 1994), p. 27.
3. Kenneth Gangel, *Feeding and Leading* (Wheaton: Victor, 1989), p. 31.

2. *Goals.* The goals of the church should develop from and in turn give support to the mission statement of the church. A goal is more specific, short range, and temporary than the mission statement. It asks the question, "How can we fulfill our mission?" Goals are the means used to effectively fulfill the mission. Goals help the church to measure progress and evaluate ministry as well as to plan and prepare for the future. Without goals, leaders will find it nearly impossible to facilitate change and bring improvement.

3. *Action plan.* The action plan is the detailed step-by-step process to fulfill the goals. The action plan is the workhorse of the organization. Action plans answer the following questions: *Who* will do it? *What* will they do? *When* will they do it? *Where* will they do it? In what *order* will they do it? What *resources* are available for doing it?

B. ELABORATION OF THE ORGANIZATIONAL FACTORS

1. *Mission.* Before the church can function well, its mission must be known. Without a mission statement, the tendency is to flounder in ministries with a great uncertainty of what needs to be done or how it should be done. Often a church will engage in many programs, services, and ministries before the reason for existence is clearly and precisely known. Therefore many congregations are confused and frustrated with contemporary church life. A church without a clear mission statement finds it far more difficult to make sure and solid decisions.

To determine the mission of a church, a study must be made in two areas. First, the Word of God must be studied in order to understand the basic reason for the church's existence. But second, a study needs to be made of the local community and the world at large. The Word of God insures the validity of the mission statement, and a knowledge of the community insures the relevancy of the mission statement. The elders and deacons, as the spiritual leaders of the church, must be the catalyst in writing a mission statement. The congregation, of course, can have input in the process. Once the mission is determined, ownership is maintained through continual review and restatement of the mission statement. One author states,

> Any leader who doesn't constantly repeat the essence of the vision, perhaps in different words, will find the people straying. The purpose must be repeated and repeated and repeated, because it gives meaning to the organization, it produces intensity and direction.[4]

An effective mission statement relates the mission of the entire church, not just the mission of the leaders. Any regular attender should be able to articulate the gist of the church's mission. The mission statement should be short and to the point, no more than a paragraph in length.

2. *Goals.* The mission statement is a broad overview of the purpose of the church. It may change little or not at all from year to year. However, the goals will change, as each year the leaders must ask, "What should we do now or in the near

---

4. Fred Smith, *Learning to Lead* (Waco, Tex.: Word, 1986), p. 36.

63

future to fulfill this mission?" Goals break the mission statement down to smaller functional units. Action plans break the goals down even further, providing step-by-step procedures and accountability. In writing goals, as many as possible of the following tests should be met.[5]

It is mission directed (helps fulfill the mission).
It is desirable (meets congregational needs).
It is conceivable (can be clearly understood).
It is attainable (it can be done).
It is measurable (it will be known when it is reached).
It is assignable (it can be delegated).
It is controllable (a limited amount of unintentional consequences).

3. *Action Plans.* Action plans, too, must be specific, measurable, and attainable. Thomas Stevenin has correctly noted that "the more unmeasurable the goal, the more measurable must be the action plan. If both a goal and an action plan are unmeasurable, we are talking nonsense." For example, leaders might have as a goal for the coming year: "to have our congregation become more spiritual." Although that is a worthy goal, it cannot be easily measured. You cannot say "to have our congregation become more spiritual by 15 percent." Since that goal cannot be measured easily, there must be a number of specific points in the action plan. If the action plan is vague, then the wording of the goal must be rethought.

C. EXAMPLES OF THE ORGANIZATIONAL FACTORS.

The following is an example of how a goal should be stated.[6]

FORMAT FOR A GOAL

To have _____ _____
             (Verb)   (Subject)

by _____ no later than _____
   (Standard [number or percentage])   (Deadline)

Example: To have increased to twelve the number of small group Bible studies no later than March 31.

The following is an example of how a mission statement, a goal, and an action plan might be interrelated.

1. *Mission Statement.* Our church exists to provide followers of Jesus Christ opportunities for corporate worship; to be equipped to serve Christ through biblical instruction and training; to provide opportunities for this body of believers to pray, fellowship, and care for one another; and to communicate God's plan of salvation to those who are not believers.

5. Lloyd Perry and Norman Shawchuck, *Revitalizing the 20th Century Church* (Chicago: Moody, 1982), p. 34.
6. Francis W. Grubbs, *Seminar Notes* (Redding, Calif.: Simpson College, n.d.).

2. *Goal.* To have increased to twelve the number of small group Bible studies no later than March 31. (Note: This goal could relate to a couple of different parts of this mission statement, depending on what specifically these small group Bible studies were set up to accomplish.)

3. *Action Plan.* (a) Jim Smith will recuit five new Bible study leaders by July 1. (b) Jim Smith and Tom Miller will train these leaders using the workbook *How to Lead Small Groups,* by Charles Lindstrom. Completed by October 1. (c) Pastor Hofstra will preach a message in September on the need for fellowship and Bible study in the Christian life. (d) The publications committee led by Tim James will print a sign-up sheet for use in recruiting during the month of October.

Other matters would also be addressed in the action plan. But this gives the general idea.

APPLICATIONAL ASSIGNMENT:

In light of the material just given, write out the mission statement of your church. (If you don't have one, this should be a priority of the church leadership.) Then, based on the mission statement, or one that you make up, formulate two goals for the next year as you look at the needs of your church. And finally, write an action plan for reaching each of these two goals.

Mission Statement: _____

_____

_____

_____

Goal #1: _____

_____

_____

Action Plan: _____

_____

_____

_____

_____

Goal #2: _____

_____

_____

Action Plan: _____

_____

_____

_____

_____

IV. THE IMPLEMENTATION OF CHURCH ORGANIZATION

A. JOB DESCRIPTIONS

When the leaders have guided the church in the adoption of a mission statement and when they have provided a yearly procedure to establish goals and action plans, the next step is a study of the delegation and organization of the work of the church. When a mission statement has been adopted, the next important step is to write down detailed job descriptions for the various jobs in the church. A worthy goal is that each worker have a written job description. It is particularly important that the church leadership have job descriptions.

In writing a job description several factors come into play:

Applicable Scripture passages

Specific needs and expectations of the local church

Guidelines from the church's bylaws and constitution

Governmental regulations

In the job description itself, certain matters must be included:

Accountability: To whom does the worker directly report?

Qualifications: What are the requirements for this position?

Selection and term: How is one appointed to this position and how long is the individual expected to serve?

Responsibilities: What exactly is the worker expected to do in this position?

B. POLICY AND PROCEDURE MANUALS

An important working document is the policy and procedure manual. In the work of the elders and deacons certain decisions or discussions seem to come up with regularity. These repetitious discussions could be done away with or at least shortened through a policy and procedure manual. This manual would list policies regarding certain decisions and procedures for various ministries or programs. Following is a brief list of some of the areas that could be listed in such a manual.

Benevolence policies (funerals, weddings, showers, food pantry)
Home Bible study guidelines
Equipment use guidelines
Copyright/Duplication policies
Kitchen rules
Nursery guidelines
Scholarship policies (camp, retreats, Bible college)

Reimbursement for workers
Worker standards
Committee appointments

A warning note must be sounded regarding the use of a policy and procedure manual. If such a manual is used, it is wise to remember that it is a tool, not a taskmaster. The manual is not inspired and must not be used to put the leaders in bondage. The manual could be reviewed and updated on a yearly basis.

C. BOARD MEETINGS

One of the greatest time savers in the work of leadership is a pre-printed agenda. This should be distributed at least two or three days prior to the meeting, thus giving leaders an opportunity to review and study the matters that will be faced in the upcoming meeting. Along with the printed agenda, any pertinent reports or fact sheets should be included. Any information that can be distributed before the meeting will shorten the decision-making process.

THE BIBLICAL IDEALS FOR CHURCH LEADERS

SESSION 6:
DELEGATION AND MOTIVATION

I. DELEGATION OF RESPONSIBILITY

In most churches with an elder-rule form of government or a congregational form of government, the elders (or board) have the majority of oversight of the church's ministry. It is to these that most workers, officers, and committee members are accountable. In a sense, the success or failure of the church rests on the shoulders of the elders (or board). However, such a burden is too much for even a large board to carry. It is necessary, therefore, that work, responsibility, and authority be delegated to others.

PREPARATORY ASSIGNMENT:

In Exodus 18 we find an excellent illustration of the need to share the load of leadership. Read Exodus 18:13-27 and respond to the following questions.

What was Moses' problem? _____

_____

What was Jethro's basic solution to that problem? _____

_____

What would probably have happened if Moses had not heeded the word of Jethro?

_____

_____

What was true of those men who were chosen to assist Moses? _____

_____

A. THE MEANING OF DELEGATION

Delegation means that we commit certain responsibilities and powers to another person, who then functions as our representative. Several key matters need to be noted. First, responsibility to perform a job or function is given. It now becomes another person's function. Second, authority must be granted in order to fulfill the delegated responsibility. The power to make certain decisions must be part of the delegation process. Third, delegation includes accountability. Two things must be clear to each individual: To whom he is accountable, and What are the standards of performance.

It has been suggested by many that delegation is not a logical issue, it is an emotional one. Leaders do not sit down and logically arrive at the conclusion that they should not delegate responsibility to others. In fact, it is almost universally conceded that it is the thing to do.

Why do you think many leaders fail to delegate responsibility to others even when they theoretically believe it the best thing to do?

_____

_____

_____

B. SOME OBSERVATIONS ON DELEGATION

From Exodus 18 and from practical experience, certain truths about delegating responsibility can be observed.

Delegation is essential for the survival of the church and the leader. One of the quickest ways to insure stress and burnout is to refuse to delegate.

Delegation is important in leadership development. One of the finest means of developing people is to give them those responsibilities that they can handle and grow in.

Delegate only to those who are qualified. It is foolish to give responsibility to just anyone. Wise leaders select the right people. The spiritual maturity and gifts of the individual must be known.

Delegate everything you can; do only what cannot be delegated. Don't do something that someone else can do. There are plenty of jobs that others cannot or will not do.

Delegation does not remove the leader from responsibility. A certain responsibility always rests on the delegator. The leader must follow up, checking on the needs and progress of the one who was given the responsibility.

C. BASIC GUIDELINES FOR DELEGATION

Perhaps one reason leaders fail to delegate is simply that they are not really sure how they should go about it. Listed below are nine guidelines that need to be considered in delegation.

The leader should recognize his own limits. This is the starting point. Unless the leader does not believe that he cannot do everything or do it well, he will not delegate. He must remember that other parts of the body can function better in some areas.

The leader should determine what needs to be delegated. He needs to note what jobs he must be freed from in order to perform best his primary responsibilities.

The leader should determine why the task is to be delegated. Some jobs will be delegated to give him more time; others will be delegated to sharpen the skills of another person. Still others may be delgated to show recognition.

The leader should match the person with the delegated task. Who would be best suited for this task? What gifts are involved? Who has shown interest in this area of service? Who will have the time to devote to it? These and other questions need to be considered before delegating.

The leader should exhibit confidence in the person selected. *How* the task is assigned is important. Does the leader express both confidence and high expectation, or does he communicate the idea that "you are my last hope, since I couldn't get anyone else."

The leader should define clearly his expectations. Unclear objectives are deadly and insure failure. Different people may have different thoughts and expectations related to an area or service. Here is where a job description is needed so that everyone views the job in a similar way.

The leader should clearly define the boundaries of authority. A great deal of frustration or animosity can develop if there is no agreement on what the person can or cannot do.

The leader should provide the needed resources for the task. The resources may include money, necessary information, training, or access to certain people or equipment.

The leader should follow up. Regular meetings or some system for adequate responding must be set up, such as the form given here.

Name _____

Date _____ Project due date _____

Project _____

To whom accountable _____

Present status of the project:

Problems I am encountering:

Additional resources that I need:

Additional notes or comments:

D. REVEALING QUESTIONS ABOUT DELEGATION

How well do you delegate responsibility? Listed below are some questions that will help in determining your effectiveness in delegation.[1] As you look at these, ask yourself if you are satisfied or dissatisfied with what you have done.

1. Kenneth Gangel, *Feeding and Leading* (Wheaton: Victor, 1989) pp. 183-84.

70

Have I been successful in retaining an effective staff?

Am I exploring and discovering the gifts and talents of my staff?

Am I effectively using both professional and lay leadership resources?

Are people demonstrating spiritual and professional growth under my leadership?

Do I take time daily to relax and think creatively?

Am I able to leave my leadership role for periods of time with the assurance that the work will go on well?

Am I discovering new leaders in the organization?

Do my subordinates delegate effectively?

II. MOTIVATION FOR SERVICE

In the ultimate sense, leaders do not motivate people to live godly lives and serve Jesus Christ. Leaders cannot legislate these things. It is the Holy Spirit who really motivates believers. But a leader can do certain things to assist the process. The apostle Paul provides an example of one who created an excellent climate for the Holy Spirit to motivate people to service and godliness.

A. PAUL MOTIVATED PEOPLE BY RECALLING BLESSINGS
   (Read Eph. 4:17-24; Rom. 12:1-2; 1 Cor. 6:9-11.)

Why is a reminder of our past condition and the power and purposes of God helpful in motivating us? _____

_____

_____

B. PAUL MOTIVATED PEOPLE BY HONEST ENCOURAGEMENT
   (Read 1 Thess. 1:2-10; 2 Thess. 1:3.)

Since positive reinforcement is a key element in motivating others, leaders need to be actively engaged in honest and insightful encouragement. Why is positive reinforcement such a strong motivator? _____

_____

_____

C. PAUL MOTIVATED PEOPLE BY PERSONAL EXAMPLE
   (Read Phil. 3:17; 4:9; 2 Cor. 1:12; 1 Cor. 4:16; 1 Thess. 3:7, 9.)

What were some areas in which Paul provided a personal example for the Christians of his day? _____

_____

_____

D. PAUL MOTIVATED PEOPLE BY STEADFAST LOVE
   (Read 1 Cor. 9:3-18; 11:20-21; 2 Cor. 4:5; 1 Thess. 2:7, 11.)

   What were some characteristics of Paul's love? _____

   _____

   _____

STUDY AREA 3
The Evangelistic Work of Church Leaders

One of the last written statements made by the apostle Paul was an exhortation to Timothy to "do the work of an evangelist. . ." (2 Tim. 4:5). Evangelism is an essential ministry of the church, and leaders are to provide leadership in this area as well. And, in order to provide that needed leadership, elders and deacons must understand the basic concepts and practices of evangelism.

Christians are called upon to communicate the gospel, or "good news." But what is the gospel? What are its essential elements? Why are we to make it known? These and related matters need to be clear to the leaders of the church.

TEXT FOR THIS STUDY AREA:

Charles C. Ryrie. *So Great Salvation*. Wheaton, Ill. Victor, 1989.

SESSION 1:
DEFINITION AND RATIONALE

PREPARATORY ASSIGNMENT:

As part of your preparation for this session, please read chapters 1-3 and 14 of *So Great Salvation*.

A definition of terms is important in any field of study, and it is extremely important to the study of evangelism. In this session we will study the various definitions of evangelism and then propose a definition that is the most effective for church leaders.

Before we begin, write down your definition of evangelism.

Evangelism is _____

_____

_____

_____

We evangelize because of the Great Commission, that command of Christ given in the four gospels and the book of Acts. Please fill in the following chart after reading the five passages (note that not all passages will have answers to the six questions).

PASSAGE	BY WHOSE AUTHORITY?	TO WHAT EXTENT?	WITH WHAT POWER?	WHAT IS THE MESSAGE?	BY WHOSE AUTHORITY?	WHAT IS THE TASK?
Matthew 28:16-20						
Mark 16:14-18						
Luke 24:44-49						
John 20:19-23						
Acts 1:6-11						

Summarize the plan of evangelism that is found in Acts 1:6-11. _____

_____

_____

I. DIFFERENT APPROACHES TO EVANGELISM

Over the years a number of different approaches to and views of evangelism have been set forth. Peter Wagner has summarized many of these into three types, or definitions, of evangelism.[1]

A. PROCLAMATION EVANGELISM

The concept involved here is to "to tell them the gospel." The emphasis is on the message, which is that salvation comes through the finished work of Jesus Christ. Those who hold to this approach believe the job is done when the gospel is proclaimed.

B. PERSUASION EVANGELISM

The emphasis here is to "win them." Those who hold to this view believe that until a person is converted, baptized, and a member of the local church, he is not really evangelized.

C. PRESENCE EVANGELISM

"Help them" is the main thrust of this position. The emphasis is on social action. Those who hold to this view believe that evangelism takes place through actions, as care is given for the physical, emotional, and social needs of people. Jesus Christ is presented incarnationally in the action of the believer.

Although some good points can be found in each view, all seem to fall short in providing an adequate working definition of evangelism. For example, those who hold to the proclamation concept do not go far enough. Yes, the lost must be told the good news, but they must also be invited and encouraged to receive Jesus Christ as Savior.

Those who believe in persuasion evangelism go too far. They have mixed evangelism and discipleship. Evangelism provides the new birth experience, whereas discipleship is the process of taking that new baby in Christ on to spiritual maturity.

Those in the presence evangelism position do not provide a clear message of God's saving grace in the cross of Christ. They do not seek or expect a decision. It almost seems that they believe in a spiritual osmosis, that by Christians being in the world, the world will somehow become Christian.

D. PETITION EVANGELISM

There is, however, a fourth type of evangelism that can be called petition evangelism. This view states that we are to "tell them and invite them." The gospel of Jesus Christ must be declared, but the unbeliever must also be invited to receive the gift of salvation.

One of the definitions of evangelism is this: Communicating the good news of Jesus Christ to unbelievers with the intent of inviting them to faith in Jesus Christ, as

1. Peter Wagner, quoted by G. Michael Cocoris, Graduate School, Moody Bible Institute, March 16, 1987.

the first step in discipleship and spiritual maturity. Note the emphasis of evangelism as a first step. The goal of evangelism is not just to have a long list of converts but to have sons and daughters in the Lord who have been brought to maturity. The goal, or result, of evangelism is not just conversion but discipleship. As seen in the study of the Great Commission, Christ commands believers to make disciples, not just converts.

It should also be observed that three persons are always involved in the process of evangelism, namely, the evangelist, the hearer, and the Holy Spirit. The evangelist proclaims the message and seeks an acceptance of it, but the hearer must respond to the message through faith. However, it is the Holy Spirit who convicts and is the "divine catalyst" for saving faith.

II. DIFFERENT REASONS FOR EVANGELISM

A major issue is, Why evangelize? There are actually a number of reasons that believers engage in evangelism.

A. SECONDARY REASONS

1. *The new personal experience of the believer.* A new convert is excited about his or her conversion experience. Spontaneously the convert witnesses to friends, relatives, and co-workers. This will usually last for thirty to ninety days, until the new believer experiences opposition or the excitement wears off.

2. *The involvement in a training program.* Many older Christians will evangelize when they have been trained and assigned to share the gospel. The problem is that people do what is expected and what they are held accountable for. When the training program is over, then the accountability ceases, and most often the evangelism does too.

3. *The motivation of guilt.* Many evangelize because of guilt. They do not want to be responsible for anyone's going to hell as a result of that person's not hearing the gospel. This will often motivate a person to witness to close friends and relatives.

These three reasons may have some validity to them, but all are inadequate. They lack a consistent motivation for evangelism. There are a number of biblical reasons believers should evangelize.

B. PRIMARY REASONS

1. *The command from God* (Matt. 28:16-20; Mark 16:14-18; Luke 24:44-49). The primary motivation for evangelism is obedience to God's command to go. As one studies the six accounts of the Great Commission this becomes very clear.

The Great Commission has always been the chief motivation for missions, cross-cultural evangelism. The command to go is clear. The seriousness of God's command must be realized. It is not the "Great Suggestion" but rather the "Great Commission." The believer evangelizes because God has commanded him to. Other reasons for evangelism are important, but this command stands alone as the supreme issue.

2. *The terrible fate of man* (Luke 16:19-28; Rev. 20:11-15). Although it is true that the main reason for evangelism is the command of God, it is also true that the horrors of eternal punishment in the lake of fire cannot be ignored as a significant motivation for evangelism.

Jesus tells the story of a rich man and a beggar in Luke 16:19-28. While the rich man lived in luxury, the beggar lived in misery and poverty. The rich man had no concern about his destiny. That changed dramatically when he died and went to hell. Hell is described by the Lord as a place where there is conscious torment and irreversible separation from God. It is a place to be avoided. The Scriptures teach that hell will be placed in the lake of fire and that from that place there is no escape for all of eternity. Eternal punishment is a reality and is obviously a serious matter. It is necessary to be about the business of evangelism because people will be separated from God in a place of torment forever if they do not have an opportunity to hear the gospel and respond to it in faith.

3. *The deep need of man* (Acts 16:6-10). The apostle Paul received a vision of a man from Macedonia begging him to come there and help them. The lost of the world are looking for something to satisfy their deep, inward longings. Even though they may not be aware of it, they are waiting for someone to bring this to them. They need the message of God brought to them. Daily they hear the bad news of this world system, and they long to hear the good news that Christians have to give. Frank Tillapaugh says, "We in the evangelical church have a commodity necessary to unstable society. We have people who understand absolutes and live by unchanging values. Even our strugglers are miles ahead of the average unchurched person."[2]

Paul describes the person without Christ in Ephesians 2:1-13. The unsaved man is separated from God, disobedient to God, living in hopeless despair, and living under the burden of sin. He needs this glorious, liberating gospel of Christ.

4. *The love of Jesus Christ* (2 Cor. 5:14-20). Believers in Jesus Christ are His ambassadors sent to proclaim His message of reconciliation. "Christ's love compels" men to give witness of the saving knowledge of Christ. When the love of Christ and the joy of salvation are experienced, the desire is for others to experience the same thing.

DISCUSSION QUESTION:

Are people who have never heard the gospel really without hope for salvation; are they lost?

_____

_____

_____

---

2. Frank Tillapaugh, *Unleashing the Church* (Ventura, Calif.: Regal, 1982), p. 64.

SESSION 2:
MESSAGE AND MEANING

Four important questions must be answered when one is studying the topic of evangelism. The first two were raised in the last session, namely, What is evangelism? and, Why do we evangelize? In this session we will focus on the question, What is the message of evangelism? The next session will deal with the question of how one goes about the work of evangelism.

PREPARATORY ASSIGNMENT:

In preparation for this session read chapters 2-4 in *So Great Salvation*.

The gospel has sometimes been referred to as the "simple gospel." And while it is true that it is simple, it is also true that there is still much confusion and debate among Christians as to what needs to be included in a complete gospel presentation. Two major fallacies regarding this subject are in operation in the church today. Some persons present a diluted gospel, omitting important aspects of it, whereas others, for a variety of reasons, add requirements to the gospel.

To gain a clearer understanding of the gospel, four important terms must be understood: *gospel, sin, repentance*, and *faith*. A study of these terms will provide the outline for this session. But first, take a minute and write out your basic gospel presentation in twenty-five words or less. Suppose a man is dying, and you have a minute to communicate the gospel. What would you say? What are the basics that you believe you would need to communicate? _____

_____

_____

_____

From Ryrie's discussion in chapter 2 of *So Great Salvation*, summarize why the words we use in presenting the gospel are very important.

_____

_____

_____

I. WHAT IS "THE GOSPEL"?

In our textbook, Charles Ryrie gives a basic but helpful reminder of the main issue in reference to the gospel.

Some of the confusion regarding the meaning of the Gospel today may arise from failing to clarify the issue involved. The issue is, How can my sins be forgiven? What is it that bars me from heaven? What is it that prevents my having eternal life? The answer is sin. Therefore, I need some way to resolve that problem. And God declares that the death of His son provides forgiveness of my sin. "Christ died for our sins"—that's as plain as it could possibly be. Sinners need a Savior.[1]

The Greek term for the gospel (*euangellon*) is a term for good news—any good news. However, as it is used by Christians, it is in reference to the good news of Jesus Christ. Even that is quite broad, for the message of Jesus Christ presents several aspects of good news. Specifically *the* gospel refers to the good news that Christ has provided salvation. We often refer to this as the gospel of the grace of God. The Great Commission commands that this gospel be preached. It is also this gospel that is emphasized by Paul in his letters.

> Paul gives us the precise definition of the Gospel we preach today in 1 Corinthians 15:3-8. The Gospel is the good news about the death and resurrection of Christ. He died and He lives—this is the content of the Gospel. The fact of Christ's burial proves the reality of His death. He did not merely swoon only to be revived later. He actually died for our sins. The inclusion of a list of witnesses proves the reality of His resurrection. He died for our sins and was buried (proof of His death); He rose and was seen by many witnesses, the majority of whom were still alive when Paul wrote 1 Corinthians (the proof of His resurrection). This same twofold content of the good news appears again in Romans 4:25: He "was delivered up . . . and was raised" (NASB). Everyone who believes in that good news is saved, for that truth, and that alone, is the Gospel of the grace of God (1 Corinthians 15:2).[2]

Paul, in 1 Corinthians, presents his basic definition of the gospel. This is the gospel that he preached. It contained the two elementary truths that Christ died for our sins and that Christ rose from the dead.

These are the basic facts of the gospel. However, it is important also to understand why it was necessary for Christ to die and rise again. Three significant words need to be studied at this point.

II. WHAT IS "SIN"?

The most common word for sin in the New Testament is the Greek word *hamartia* (e.g., John 1:29; 1 John 1:7-8; Rom. 3:9; 5:12, 21; 6:1). It literally means "to miss the mark." When we sin, we are missing the mark of God's righteous standard. But we are at the same time, of course, hitting something else, namely, unrighteousness. And man often deliberately aims at and hits unrighteousness. That is why other New Testament words include the idea of rebellion, wickedness, and lawlessness when referring to the sin of man.

What insights about sin can be found in these verses?

1 John 3:4 _____

Romans 5:12 _____

Psalm 51:4 _____

Isaiah 53:6 _____

1. Charles Ryrie, So *Great Salvation* (Wheaton, Ill.; Victor 1989), p. 40.
2. Ibid., p. 39.

Romans 8:6-8 _____

Matthew 15:18-20 _____

John 8:43-44 _____

Galatians 5:17-21 _____

In presenting the concept of sin to an unbeliever, two key verses need to be discussed. The first of these is Romans 3:23, which states that "all have sinned and fall short of the glory of God." "All" indicates that sin is a universal malady of mankind. Everyone is included. Sin is said to be a falling short of God's glory, which has reference to God's holiness or standards of perfection. Falling short indicates that there is a requirement that is set before mankind. The standard God sets for man is God Himself. Jesus told the people of His day that they had to be perfect just as the heavenly Father is perfect (Matt. 5:48). In discussing sin with an unbeliever it is important to bring him to the point of recognizing God's absolute standard and that, as a man, he has fallen short of that standard. Jesus Christ becomes an excellent example of God's standard. Sometimes it might be helpful to use the Ten Commandments to convince people of their sin.

The second verse that needs to be discussed is Romans 6:23, which states that "the wages of sin is death, but the gift of God is eternal life in Christ Jesus our Lord." This verse can be applied to the unsaved person because it clearly presents the scriptural truth that sin brings about separation. Essentially, death is separation. Physical death separates the body from the soul. Spiritual death brings a separation from God. Sin separates man from God; thus he feels empty, purposeless, and lonely. Man tries to remove that separation through many means but without success. The bad news is that all have sinned, and this sin leads to death, which is eternal separation from God. This issue of man's sinfulness has been removed or downplayed in many modern presentations of the gospel. But man's sin and lost condition are key elements in the gospel message.

When the bad news of sin has been presented and is clearly understood, then the good news—the gospel—can be presented: Christ died for our sins, and He rose again from the dead.

Briefly summarize the basic truths regarding sin:

What is sin? _____

Who has sinned? _____

What is the consequence of sin? _____

What is the remedy for sin? _____

II. WHAT IS "REPENTANCE"?

Based on chapter 9 of *So Great Salvation*, answer the following questions.
What is the basic meaning of repentance?

_____

_____

What three ways does the New Testament use the word *repentance*?

_____

_____

How did Peter use the word *repent* in Acts 2:38? _____

What is it that people are to repent about? _____

_____

What is the relationship between repentance and saving faith?_____

_____

_____

Sinners dead in trespasses and sin many times have wrong thinking that must be corrected and changed. In evangelism it is important to ferret out wrong beliefs, graciously and tactfully refute them, and replace them with the teaching of the Word of God. Repentance can come only after God's truth is presented as a valid alternative for faulty reasoning.

It is important to remember that there is a difference between repentance and the fruits of repentance. Repentance, as a requirement for salvation, is a change of mind about Jesus Christ—that He is the one and only savior from sin. The fruit of repentance follows salvation and is part of the new birth of sanctifying work of the Holy Spirit. "Biblical repentance also involves changing one's mind in a way that effects some change in the person. Repentance is not merely an intellectual assent to something; it also includes a resultant change, usually in actions."[3]

Ephesians 2:8 declares that "it is by grace you have been saved, through faith." Faith, in this verse, also includes repentance. Both faith and repentance are a decision of the mind and the will. If repentance is defined as a change in action, it then becomes work. And that is not compatible with biblical teaching. It is true, of course, that change in action and behavior should take place in the life of one who has accepted Jesus Christ as Savior. But this is a result of salvation and not a prerequisite for it.

IV. WHAT IS "FAITH"?

After reading chapter 11 in *So Great Salvation*, answer the following questions.

Why does Ryrie suggest that believing in Jesus Christ is not easy? _____

_____

_____

What are the three basic elements of faith? _____

_____

_____

What is a good definition of saving faith? _____

_____

_____

Who is the object of faith?_____

_____

3. Ibid., p. 92

What place does commitment have in trusting Christ for salvation? _____

_____

_____

Michael Cocoris states that faith is the most important issue in salvation.[4] The unbeliever must have a proper understanding of the gospel, sin, and repentance. But without faith this proper understanding is only head knowledge. Faith acts upon that knowledge and receives and believes God's Word.

Warren Wiersbe gives this definition of faith. "True Bible faith is *confident obedience* to God's word in spite of circumstances and consequences. This faith operates quite simply. God speaks and we hear His word. We *trust* His word and *act* on it no matter what.[5]

Michael Cocoris's summary of faith is mental assent and reliance based on the knowledge of God's word.[6]

Essential to saving faith are these truths:

Jesus Christ is fully God and fully man. Only by being the sinless Son of God, who was tempted in all points as man is, could He pay the price for sin. He is the one and only savior of mankind (John 20:31; 1 John 4:2).

Man is a sinner, and sin has separated him from God (Rom. 3:23; 6:23).

Man can do nothing to merit salvation (Eph. 2:8-9).

Jesus Christ died for man's sin and rose again, signifying that the payment for sin was accepted by God (1 Cor. 15:1-5).

The responsibility of the evangelist is to present this knowledge to the unbeliever, dealing patiently and tactfully with any questions or objections. But this knowledge must be accepted or believed as true and appropriated by the unbeliever in order for salvation to take place. Evangelism has not taken place until the unbeliever has been given the essential truths about sin and the person and work of Christ and has been asked to believe in Jesus Christ. When dealing with an unbeliever, it is vital to be certain that the object of faith is Jesus Christ. Faith is based on the Person and work of Jesus Christ as revealed in God's word. Faith in anyone or anything else will not save.

CONCLUDING ASSIGNMENT:

In light of our study of the content of evangelism, complete the following assignment. To summarize the truths discussed in this section, write out a brief evangelistic presentation. Include the concepts of the gospel, sin, repentance, and faith. Imagine that a child in the junior department (ages 9-12) has come to you and asked, "How can I be saved?"

_____

_____

_____

4. Cocoris, *Evangelism: A Biblical Approach* (Michael Cocoris, P.O. Box 233, South Pasadena, CA 91031), p. 73.
5. Warren Wiersbe, *Be Confident* (Wheaton, Ill.: Victor, 1983), pp. 120-21.
6. Cocoris, p. 76.

SESSION 3:
GUIDELINES AND METHODS

One distinguishing mark of a spiritual leader is a burden that the unsaved person would come to know Jesus Christ as the Savior. This burden leads the spiritual leader to a verbal expression of faith in Christ, giving a witness to the life-changing experience of salvation and cleansing from sin, and inviting others to receive God's gift of salvation. Most spiritual leaders want to be effective witnesses for Christ. The attendance at the various evangelism training seminars attest to that fact. But even with the many tools and training available today, most Christians are somewhat embarrassed about their attempts or lack of attempts at evangelism. Sometimes the embarrassment even leads to hopelessness and defeat, so that they view themselves as complete failures at evangelism. That need not be the case.

PREPARATORY ASSIGNMENT:

      For this session answer the following questions based on the suggested Scripture passages.

According to Ephesians 4:11-13, whom does God use to evangelize? _____

_____

According to the following Scripture texts, what five things should we pray for as we evangelize?

Matthew 9:37-38 _____

Colossians 4:3 _____

Acts 4:29-30 _____

1 Timothy 2:1-3 _____

According to 1 Thessalonians 2:1-8, what are two major reasons for the boldness of the apostle Paul?_____

_____

_____

Based on Acts 8:26-39, list at least three biblical principles for presenting the gospel.

_____

_____

_____

After reading Acts 2:37-42, list five follow-up activities of a new believer:

_____   _____

_____   _____

_____

DISCUSSION QUESTION:

How does "common sense" have a bearing on evangelism?

_____

_____

_____

I. SOME BIBLICAL GUIDELINES FOR EVANGELISM

Any believer can witness. The patterns for evangelism found in the Bible can be helpful in bringing us to the place where we are effective witnesses for Christ. Guidelines for evangelism may be found in several Scriptures. For this study, the guidelines for evangelism taken from the life of Philip the evangelist will be viewed. Philip was a layman, selected as one of the men who had to deal with the first major problem in the new church (Acts 6:1-6). Later, in Acts 8, he is seen preaching in a city of Samaria. As a result of his ministry a great spiritual awakening took place and many people believed and were baptized.

Shortly after this, the Jerusalem church sent Peter and John to investigate these events in Samaria. In the midst of this significant awakening, Philip received a message from God to go to a lonely desert road. He did not know the reason for this geographic change but soon learned that God wanted him to evangelize an important official from Ethiopia. From the story of Philip, six truths can be applied to our personal evangelism.[1] (Review this story by reading all of Acts 8.)

A. BE SENSITIVE (ACTS 8:26)

Philip could have been so caught up in the excitement of what was happening that he was not sensitive to a new direction. But Philip was alert to God's message. Michael Cocoris emphasizes the importance of prayer in the preparation, presentation, and follow-up of evangelism. Philip seems to have recognized this need and appears to have been in prayer. The message that God gave to Philip seems to be ill-advised. Why leave a responsive community to go to a desert road? God sometimes may ask His people to do the unexpected without explanation. As we witness for Christ, we must be sensitive and prayerful so that we can be led by the Spirit.

B. BE AVAILABLE (ACTS 8:27-29)

Philip did not struggle or debate with God. He obeyed and as a result was God's man for that hour. God had been preparing the heart of a man from Ethiopia. The Ethiopian had been to Jerusalem to worship and as he headed for home was sitting in his chariot reading the Word of God. He had many questions and was ripe for someone to explain the gospel to him. Philip was available for that task. It is important to note

1. Charles Swindoll, *Strengthening Your Grip* (Waco, Tex.: Word), 1982, pp. 226ff.

that God is concerned about the salvation of one person. Evangelism is winning the lost one person at a time. We do not know when God will direct us to speak to some unsaved person about the Lord. We need to be sure that we are available to Him as Philip was.

C. TAKE THE INITIATIVE (ACTS 8:30)

Philip took the initiative in establishing a conversation with the man from Ethiopia by asking a simple question. Questions are an excellent approach to begin building a bridge to an unbeliever. Michael Cocoris says:

> Whether you provide a question with your life-style or pose a question with your lips, the transition from a secular to a spiritual conversation is the question. The question is the line of demarcation. Once you cross it, it is easier to go ahead than to go back.[2]

All of the contemporary evangelistic programs use the question to begin a conversation or to make a transition in conversation. It is a time-honored and proven method. The following questions suggested by Charles Swindoll might prove helpful in your witnessing experiences.[3]

What do you think a real Christian is?

What do you think is wrong with the world today?

With the threat of the bomb, earthquakes, or other calamities, how do you keep from being afraid?

Who was the greatest person who ever lived? Why?

An important concept relating to taking the initiative must be considered. In the Lord's story of the sower and the seed in Matthew 13:3-9, the sower is seen going out into the field to scatter the seed. This story assumes that it is the believer's responsibility to take the initiative to sow the seed. It is quite difficult to sow the seed while staying at home. Sowing the seed is our responsibility; the results are God's responsibility.

D. BE TACTFUL (Acts 8:30-34)

Philip was not offensive in his dealings with the Ethiopian. Paul does say that the preaching of the cross will be offensive to some, but that is not an excuse for being obnoxious or tactless in the way we approach people. The messenger of the gospel must attempt to be unoffensive in his relationships and conversations with others.

In Philip's case he waited for an invitation before intruding on the man's privacy. Philip asked a question but waited for an invitation before joining the Ethiopian in the chariot. Philip did take the initiative, but he did so with sensitivity and patience.

Much harm has been done to Christianity by overzealous, obnoxious "salesmen" of the gospel. No one appreciates a pushy salesman who threatens and appears selfish and uncaring. Beware of pushing yourself on others, even for the sake of the gospel. In the study of Christ's style of personal evangelism, it is apparent that He never forced Himself on anyone.

2. Cocoris, *Evangelism: A Biblical Approach* (Michael Cocoris, P.O. Box 233, South Pasadena, CA 91031), p.136.
3. Charles Swindoll, *Strengthening Your Grip* (Waco, Tex.: Word, 1982), p. 229.

Tactfulness comes by putting yourself in the other person's place. Keep in mind that an unbeliever is not coming from where we are, nor does he understand where we are going. Do not argue, but rather try to find a way to agree. For example, an individual might raise the common complaint that the church is full of hypocrites. You might defuse that complaint by saying. "Yes, I agree that there are hypocrites in the church, but would you allow me to show you what a real Christian is like?"

E. BE PRECISE (Acts 8:.34-35)

When the time was right, Philip spoke precisely and clearly about Jesus Christ. When witnessing, stay on the issue of Christ as the answer to man's problem of sin. Do not get sidetracked with unnecessary religious issues or debates. However, when valid questions or objections arise they need to be dealt with. Tactfulness does require that legitimate questions and concerns be addressed.

This study does not allow for us to discuss the many objections and questions that could arise, but several good books are available that deal with such matters.

I'm Glad You Asked, by Kenneth Boa and Larry Moody

Evidence that Demands a Verdict, by Josh McDowell

More Evidence That Demands a Verdict, by Josh McDowell

Mere Christianity, by C. S. Lewis

F. SEEK A DECISION

When it was obvious that the man from Ethiopia was ready to make a decision, Philip followed through on it. When the time seems right, seek a decision. However, do not wait indefinitely. Sometimes you may have to ask several times in one way or another: "Will you receive Jesus Christ as your Savior?" Even at this time, sensitivity and tact are important.

II. SOME METHODS OF EVANGELISM

A variety of ways may be used to present the gospel. It is important that we have a plan or basic approach that we are familiar with. Then, when witnessing to an individual, we will have a great deal more confidence in what we are doing. We will have less of a tendency to get sidetracked in our presentation of the gospel.

A. THE ROMAN ROAD

This approach focuses on Romans 3:23; 6:23; 5:8; and 10:9-10. Once the evangelist has an opportunity to share the gospel and has ascertained that the unbeliever is ready to hear the gospel, he/she proceeds to explain the basic truths that:

1. All have sinned (Rom. 3:23).

2. The penalty of sin is death (Rom. 6:27).

3. Christ died for our sins (Rom. 5:8).

4. We receive Christ's salvation through confession and belief (Rom. 10:9-10).

B. THE BILL ROBINSON APPROACH

Another helpful method is given by Bill Robinson in his book *Getting Beyond the Small Talk*, which is published by the Billy Graham Evangelistic Association. This book outlines a step-by-step approach to witnessing by using the helpful visual aid of a football field. Robinson describes it this way.

> In order to determine where God has brought people in their spiritual process, I visualize myself on a spiritual football field. I am at one end of the field on the zero-yard line. Through different conversation techniques, I am then able to determine approximately where he is in his spiritual journey. We are responsible for our half of the field—our fifty yards.[5]

In this presentation each of the ten-yard segments represents an area of conversation that is designed to lead the conversation of the individual.

> The first ten yards is general conversation. When I come off my zero-yard line with general conversation (weather, baseball), I hope he does the same. If he does, then I move from the ten-yard line to the twenty-yard line with personalized conversation topics (family, job, interests). My third level of conversation is general religious talk, (churches, Sunday school, youth group activities, and so forth). We are now between the twenty- and the thirty-yard lines.[6]

On each level of conversation, it is essential to be alert and sensitive to the responsiveness of the unbeliever. Bill Robinson observes that many Christians get frustrated and discouraged in their witnessing because they think they have to save souls "right now" and push too hard. He observes the following.

> [The] average Christian visualizes coming off the zero-yard line, going all the way down the field, past the fifty-yard line, past the forty-, thirty-, all the way to the other person's zero-yard line. He starts pressing too quickly the gospel, the Christian life, and his subject's sinful condition. Eventually he gets discouraged because he either gets nowhere, or the abruptness provokes a negative reaction.[7]

The fourth level of conversation gets into the sensitive area of personal religious issues.

> Then I go to personal religious comments, concerning myself and concerning him. I will go from talking about God generally, to what Christ has done for me or what He means to me. I will go from talking about the decline of morals generally to what the Bible says specifically. All along, I have been asking for feedback, and now I begin asking more personal questions about his views regarding his church, the Bible, God and Christ. This is the thirty- to forty-yard line. We move on toward the fifty-yard line only if the person is responding by talking, following, or involving himself in the conversation. . . . When we reach our respective forty-yard lines, I start into the gospel presentation. At this point I take it a yard at a time. I do not want to rush through the gospel. Only when he feels he is ready to trust the Lord Jesus Christ have we finally met at the fifty-yard line.[7]

5. Bill Robinson, *Getting Beyond the Small Talk* (Minneapolis: Worldwide, 1989), pp. 23-24.
6. Ibid., pp. 24-25.
7. Ibid., p. 26.

Once the point comes when the gospel is being presented, Robinson uses a modified version of the "Romans Road." Some of the other popular plans for communicating the gospel are Campus Crusade's "Four Spiritual Laws" and Billy Graham's "Steps to Peace with God."

C. EVANGELISM EXPLOSION

This author would encourage all church leaders to attend an Evangelism Explosion Training Clinic.

Their evangelism approach is based on five main points.

1. GRACE

Heaven is a free gift (Rom. 6:23).

It cannot be earned or deserved (Eph. 2:8-9).

2. MAN

Is a sinner (Rom. 3:23) and cannot save himself (Prov. 14:12).

3. GOD

Is merciful and therefore does not want to punish us (1 John 4:8).

But God is also just and must punish sin (Exod. 34:7).

4. CHRIST

Solved the problem between God's love and justice.

He is the infinite God-Man (John 1:1, 14).

He died on the cross and rose from the dead to pay the penalty for our sins and to purchase a place in heaven for us, which He offers as a free gift.

5. FAITH

Christ's free gift is received by faith, which is trusting in Jesus Christ alone for eternal life (Acts 16:31).

CONCLUDING ASSIGNMENT:

Prayerfully consider an unbelieving acquaintance with whom you could share the gospel. Seek prayer support and make plans to evangelize that person. Write down the name of the person whom you will attempt to win to Christ.

Following your evangelistic opportunity, write out a brief synopsis of the incident to share with the other members of your study group.

The Shepherding Ministries of Church Leaders

Basic to the task of the church leader is shepherding. If there is anything that he must be it is a shepherd to the people he is leading.

Our Lord's favorite metaphor for spiritual leadership, a figure He often used to describe Himself, was that of a shepherd—one who tends God's flock. Every church leader is a shepherd. The word *pastor* itself even means "shepherd." It is appropriate imagery. A shepher leads, feeds, nurtures, comforts, corrects, and protects.[1]

As those who would lead the church, God's flock, we must not see ourselves simply as administrators and decision makers but rather as those who, with great concern, lead and feed the sheep. It is the purpose of this study area to help us develop the attitude and the tools that are needed to shepherd well the flock.

TEXT FOR THIS STUDY AREA:

Michael Slater. *Becoming a Stretcher Bearer.* Ventura, Calif.: Regal, 1984.

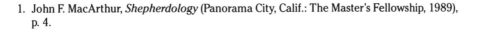

1. John F. MacArthur, *Shepherdology* (Panorama City, Calif.: The Master's Fellowship, 1989), p. 4.

THE SHEPHERDING MINISTRIES OF CHURCH LEADERS
SESSION 1:
IMPORTANCE AND EXPLANATION

PREPARATORY ASSIGNMENTS:

1. The textbook for this session is *Becoming a Stretcher Bearer,* by Michael Slater. Read chapters 1, 2, 5, 6, and 7, and briefly answer the following questions.

   Based on the story in chapter one, how would you define or describe a "stretcher bearer"? _____

   _____

   _____

   What destroys people when they find themselves on a stretcher? _____

   _____

   _____

   What is our responsibility for dealing with the main issue and secondary issues of others' problems? _____

   _____

   _____

   _____

   What are the costs of being a "stretcher bearer"? _____

   _____

   _____

   As you look at the costs, which would be the greatest cost to you personally?

   _____

   _____

   What are the key issues in a person's getting started in the ministry of "stretcher bearing"? _____

   _____

   _____

2. The Scriptures contain a great deal of truth concerning the characteristics of shepherds. Study the following passages, and discover what you can about shepherding.

The Lord Jesus is the "Good Shepherd." From John 10:1-18 and Psalm 23, list as many characteristics as you can of Christ's ministry as a shepherd. _____

_____

_____

_____

_____

Which attitudes are correct and which are unacceptable for a shepherd to have according to 1 Peter 5:1-3? _____

_____

_____

_____

_____

What responsibilities of the shepherd/elder are given in Acts 20:28-30? _____

_____

_____

_____

_____

In this session we want to center our attention on three questions: namely, What is shepherding? Why must a leader function as a shepherd? How does a leader function as a shepherd?

I. DEFINITIONS OF SHEPHERDING

The word "shepherd" in 1 Peter 5:2 is translated from the Greek word *poimano*, which basically means to care as a shepherd. A shepherd cares for his sheep by providing their basic needs of food, water, shelter, and protection. A shepherd is a picture of the spiritual care-giver in the Bible. He guides, guards, and seeks to meet the needs of those in God's flock. He "pastors" the flock.

Unfortunately the word *pastor* (shepherd) has come to mean a professional clergyman. In the thinking of most people the word refers to an office, or position. However, *pastor* in its original usage refers to the one providing for the needs of those entrusted to his care. And this may or may not be a professional clergyman. It should be clear that pastoring is not just the function of a paid pastor but is a shared responsibility of the elders, deacons, and other gifted people within the church. One writer defines pastoring as "caring for another by giving oneself in Christian love to a relationship in times of weakness and times of strength."[1]

Shepherding presupposes that people have basic needs that must be addressed and cared for within the church. Note that in this session, the terms *shepherding* and *pastoring* are used synonymously. They refer to the providing of care for the needs of individuals and congregations.

II. REASONS FOR SHEPHERDING

We will focus on three reasons for a leader's functioning as a shepherd.

A. THE COMMAND OF GOD

Earlier in this session several Scriptures were observed. In these the responsibilities of leaders were plainly given. First Peter 5:2 instructs leaders to "be shepherds of God's flock, entrusted to your care." Paul, in Acts 20:28, commands: "Keep watch over yourselves and all the flock of which the Holy Spirit has made you overseers. Be shepherds of the church of God." These commands, along with others, declare that the leaders of the local church have the God-given responsibility to care for those over whom they have been given charge.

In the Old Testament the leaders of Israel were sometimes pictured as shepherds. In an interesting verse in Ezekiel 34 the Lord speaks out against these shepherds of Israel: "Son of man, prophesy against the shepherds of Israel; prophesy and say to them: This is what the sovereign Lord says: Woe to the shepherds of Israel who only take care of themselves! Should not the shepherds take care of the flock?"

In this passage the Lord is angry that the shepherds are not doing their job. The question He asks, "Should not shepherds take care of the flock?" is rhetorical. It is preposterous to think of a shepherd who does not provide care for his flock. The remainder of Ezekiel 34 points out that the Lord will hold unfaithful shepherds accountable if they neglect their basic duty as care-givers.

B. THE PRIESTHOOD OF BELIEVERS

One great truth of the New Testament is that all believers in Christ are priests. A priest is one who represents God to the people and also represents the people to God. Every believer is to function in these ways in ministering to others and praying for others. However, church leaders have a unique privilege and responsibility to carry on the function of a priest for others. The spiritul leaders of the church must be worthy models and be diligent in this ministry.

C. THE NEEDS OF THE PEOPLE

Another argument for the necessity of shepherding is the needs of the people. Needs are everywhere and appear in a variety of ways. One well-known study of human needs suggests that there are five levels of need that all mankind possesses.[2]

Physiological needs: those things necessary to maintain life, such as food, water, oxygen, and rest.

1. Melvin J. Steinbron, *Can the Pastor Do It Alone?* (Ventura, Calif.: Regal, 1987), p. 39.
2. Abraham Maslow, quoted by H. Norman Wright in *Premarital Counseling* (Chicago: Moody, 1977), pp. 88-89.

Safety needs: a lifestyle that gives protection and avoidance of danger; a life of structure rather than disorder.

Love and belonging needs: the need for affectionate, caring relationships with other people.

Esteem needs: receiving recognition as a worthwhile person.

Self-actualization needs: becoming the person one has the potential to be.

Tied in with these psychological and physical needs are spiritual needs such as forgiveness, peace, salvation, and holiness. The spiritual leader does not need to look far to find needs that can be filled. The needs of people cry out for the care of a shepherd.

At this point a warning must be given. It is important to realize that no one shepherd can meet all the needs of his people. The leader/shepherd must exercise wisdom. He must provide care, but he cannot care for every need. Overdependence on the shepherd not only wears out the shepherd, but it produces immaturity in the person, as well as the church. Paul displays the balance that needs to be ours in Galatians 6:2 and 5: "Carry each others' burdens, and in this way you will fulfill the law of Christ . . . each one should carry his own load."

The faithful shepherd helps carry the load, while teaching the individual how to do his part.

III. SUGGESTIONS FOR SHEPHERDING

Shepherding is providing care for the needs of people entrusted to the shepherd. The ministry of shepherding must be performed because of God's command, the implication of the priesthood of believers, and the many needs of humanity. The question of "How to do?" needs to be addressed. What are some important principles of the shepherding ministry? Perhaps the following suggestions will stimulate your thinking.

A. SUGGESTIONS BY THOMAS ODEN

Thomas Oden, in his book *Pastoral Theology,* lists several personal qualities that are needed by the shepherd who is serious about his care for others.

1. *Deep insight and extensive self-knowledge.* It is important to know ourselves and to be able to understand the experiences that we have had. "To know oneself is a central premise of knowing others helpfully. The more we grasp our own experience, the better we can understand and respond to the experience of others."[3]

Unless the shepherd knows and acknowledges his own need for others, he will be of little help to others. Sometimes it is only after we have gone through a time of personal crisis that we recognize how much we truly need other people.

2. *A love for people.* Unless the shepherd truly loves people, especially the unlovable, his ministry will be cold and forced. It is important to realize that the biblical concept of love is not an emotion that comes and goes. It is rather an act of the will that produces the actions of love.

3. Thomas C. Oden, *Pastoral Theology: Essentials of Ministry* (San Francisco: Harper & Row, 1983), p. 188.

3. *Accurate empathy.* The shepherd must be able to put himself in the shoes of others. Our textbook *Becoming a Stretcher Bearer* refers to this as being creative and sensitive in response to others—creative by using imagination to devise the most appropriate ways to meet others needs and sensitive by seeing clearly the needs of others.

4. *Situational wisdom.* Situational wisdom is built on the knowledge stored in the data base of one's mind. This knowledge comes from Scripture, experience, and from education. It is that ability to speak the right word at the right time. Situational wisdom grows with age and experience. This is probably why the term *elder* means more than just spiritual maturity but also includes the idea of having life experience.

5. *Being trustworthy and trusting.* The shepherd must be trusted by those to whom he attempts to give care. Likewise, the shepherd must trust those to whom he ministers. The lack of trust destroys effective ministry.

6. *Genuineness, candor, and honesty.* A shepherd needs to be transparent and open. He must not play a role that is not really himself.

7. *Related personal characteristics.* A leader who cares must have a number of other characteristics that will aid him in being an effective care-giver. Oswald Sanders, in his classic book *Spiritual Leadership,* mentions such things as courage, humor, discipline, and patience.[4]

B. SUGGESTIONS BY JAY ADAMS

One of the factors consistently present in the Lord's earthly ministry was His care and concern for people. Jay Adams has observed nine ministries in the life of the Good Shepherd.[5]

1. *Concern for each individual sheep.* The Lord is *my* shepherd.

2. *Rest.* He makes me to lie down.

3. *Provision for daily sustenance.* He leads to green pastures and still waters.

4. *Refreshment and encouragement.* He restores my soul.

5. *Guidance and leadership.* He leads me.

6. *Instruction, training, and disciplines.* He leads in the paths of righteousness.

7. *Provision for goals and motivation.* This is done for His name's sake.

8. *Security and protection.* His rod and staff protect me.

9. *Personal fellowship and loving friendship.* He is with me.

C. SUGGESTIONS BY MEL STEINBRON

A helpful acronym used by Mel Steinbron in *Can the Pastor Do It Alone?* provides a practical outline for ministering to the needs of others. The word is P-A-C-E:

---

4. Oswald Sanders, *Spiritual Leadership* (Chicago: Moody, 1994), pp. 49-60.
5. Jay Adams, *Shepherding God's Flock* (Nutley, N.J.: Presby. and Ref., 1975), p. 6.

*P*ray for each one regularly.
Be *A*vailable.
*C*ontact each on a regular basis.
Provide a Christian *E*xample.

1. *Pray for each one regularly.* The greatest ministry that we can have for one another is that of prayer. We need to intercede for others. Not only do we present the situation of another before the loving and powerful Lord, but the very act of praying will cause us to be more alert and sensitive to their needs.

2. *Be available.* Being available requires commitment and sometimes sacrifice. It may be that our sacrifice is that of time and energy or perhaps of our resources. A shepherd needs to plan on having disruptions of his time and the tapping of his energies and resources.

3. *Contact each other on a regular basis.* Contact can be made in any number of ways and in any number of places. With our busy lives and full schedules, creativity is a key to success. The matter of contact will be discussed in greater detail in the next session.

4. *Provide a Christian example.* On a number of occasions Paul exhorted people to follow his example. He could do this legitimately because he himself was following Christ. A shepherd/leader points the way to Christ. The best way to help people see how to live and how to overcome sin and failure is to provide a living example. Paul told the Christians at Philippi to remember the things he had taught them and had seen in his life (Phil. 4:9). This combination of knowing and observing is crucial to the implementation of truth into life.

SOME QUESTIONS TO CONSIDER:

Of the four basic elements of shepherding (P-A-C-E), which one do you think is most lacking in the church today? _____

Which element do you think you will have to monitor the most in your shepherding ministry? _____

Why would that be the case? _____

_____

_____

Name one thing that your church could do to improve the shepherding ministry of its leadership. _____

_____

_____

SESSION 2:
CONTACTING AND CARING

Shepherds of the flock must have contact with those entrusted to their care. It is only through personal contact that it is possible really to understand needs and to address those needs properly. The expression of a caring attitude, which comes through personal contact, is a vital necessity. A caring ministry implies close interaction and involvement, and the Scriptures abound with references to the necessity of such personal contact.

> Religion that God our Father accepts as pure and faultless is this: to look after orphans and widows in their distress. (James 1:27)

> For I was hungry and you gave me something to eat, I was thirsty and you gave me something to drink, I was a stranger and you invited me in, I needed clothes and you clothed me, I was sick and you looked after me, I was in prison and you came to visit me . . . whatever you did for one of the least brothers of mine, you did for me. (Matt. 25:35, 36, 40)

> Share with God's people who are in need. Practice hospitality . . . . rejoice with those who rejoice; mourn with those who mourn. (Rom. 12:13, 15)

The Greek word *episkopeo*, in the passages just given, is translated by our English words "tend," "look after," and "visit." Jay Adams says that this word emphasizes "remembering or thinking about another that leads to action. To visit is to show concern for in blessing or in judgment. It is to show concern that grows out of one's oversight and inspection."[1] He goes on to say, "Thus, the idea of taking measures to inspect and attend whatever condition one discovers, out of concern, is the main thrust of the word."[2]

Many ways exist for carrying out this important task of shepherding: home visitation, hospital visitation, hospitality in the home of the leader, counseling appointments, church fellowships and services, social events, breakfast meetings, and phone calls. Leaders can use mutual hobbies or interests as a tool for contact and follow-up. The elders and deacons have a God-given responsibility to be in touch with the people entrusted to their care. Contact with people is the way to learn the needs of people and determine how best to address those needs.

PREPARATORY ASSIGNMENTS:

In preparing ourselves for discussion in the area of contact ministry there are a number of Scriptures to look at and three additional chapters out of Michael Slater's book, *Becoming a Stretcher Bearer,* to read.

---

1. Jay Adams, *Shepherding God's Flock* (Nutley, N.J.: Presby. and Ref., 1975), pp. 75-76.
2. Ibid., p. 76.

1. The Lord Jesus, the Good Shepherd, was in constant contact with people. Read the following verses from the gospels, and briefly answer the questions.

   A. Jesus had contact with people from various social and political backgrounds. He was unafraid of the prejudices of His day and met with all kinds of people. Note the backgrounds of the people in these verses.

   John 3:1-2, 10 _____   John 4:7-18 _____

   John 4:46-50 _____   Luke 7:11-15 _____

   Luke 7:36-50 _____   Luke 6:13-16 _____

   Matthew 8:5-13 _____   Matthew 12:2-6 _____

   Matthew 19:16-22 _____   Matthew 22:23, 34-35 _____

   B. Jesus did not limit himself to any one geographic area but had contact with people in many places. These people from differing areas had differing views and attitudes. Give the locations mentioned in these verses.

   Mark 5:1 _____   Mark 10:46 _____

   John 4:6 _____   Matthew 4:12-13 _____

   C. Jesus met the various needs of people. What are some of the needs mentioned in these verses?

   John 3:1-9 _____

   Matthew 8:2-4 _____

   Mark 10:35-44 _____

   John 11:4-35 _____

   Matthew 16:15-28 _____

2. Read chapters 3, 4, and 5 in *Becoming a Stretcher Bearer,* and answer the following quesitions.

   A. What four reasons do people generally have for refusing a ministry of care and help from others? (Put these in your own words.) _____

   _____

   _____

   B. What is the author's definition of "Gethsemane"? _____

   _____

   C. What three factors enabled Christ to pass through Gethsemane successfully—the elements needed in helping others through difficult times? _____

   _____

   _____

   D. From the story of the raising of Lazarus, what is the responsibility of believers? What is not the responsibility of believers? _____

As leaders enter into the area of contact ministry, several important matters should be kept in mind.

I. PRIORITIES IN CONTACT MINISTRIES

A. CRISIS NEEDY

Elders, deacons, and other spiritual leaders have many responsibilities at home, work, and church. Time is limited. Therefore, in anticipation of a contact ministry certain priorities should be established. The first is crisis situations. Crisis situations are those special needs that are so urgent that one ignores everything else in order to be of assistance. Examples of crisis situations are life threatening emergencies, death of an individual, or a sudden traumatic experience in a person's life. When it has been established that there is indeed a crisis situation, it is necessary to respond as quickly as possible.

B. SICK AND ELDERLY

The second priority in contact ministry is the visitation of the sick and elderly. They may not have immediate critical needs, but they will have spiritual and emotional needs that require attention on a regular basis. A hospital patient should be visited within two days of admittance and two or three times a week during his stay. Follow-up contact in the home is also appropriate during recovery. The elderly or those who are homebound or institutionalized should receive periodic contact, depending on their needs.

C. NON-CRISIS NEEDY

The third priority of visitation is to those within the church who have expressed a specific need or those whom the leaders recognize as having a need. These contacts may be delayed for a day or two, but response should be as soon as possible.

D. CHURCH VISITORS

The fourth priority is to visitors of church services. A follow-up letter should be sent within two days of the initial visit. If the visitor is new to the community or is unchurched, a personal contact should be made during the following week. If the visitor attends another church in the community, contact should not normally be made until the person has attended about three Sundays.

E. RELIABLE FAITHFUL

The final priority is to the healthy members of the congregation. Healthy, of course, is a relative term since often those who appear to have their lives "all together" actually have deep needs and hurts hidden below the surface. Such needs will be uncovered only during personal contact. These faithful people often need a visit for affirmation and encouragement.

Within the local church the contact ministries need to be shared by all of those in leadership. It is important to establish programs where the load will be carried by the many and not just one or two.

II. GUIDELINES FOR CONTACT MINISTRIES

When engaged in visitation or other contact ministries, we want to be as effective as possible. The following reminders will help us.

A. GENERAL GUIDELINES

1. *Contact ministries must be undergirded with prayer.*
2. *Contact ministries are an expression of love and concern.* Therefore make every effort to convey the presence and comfort of Jesus Christ.
3. *Listening is more needful than talking.* Ask appropriate questions without acting as a prosecuting attorney.
4. *Be courteous and tactful.*
5. *Practice good grooming and hygiene.*
6. *Be friendly and warm, while respecting the right of privacy.*
7. *Be aware of and avoid compromising situations.*
8. *Not every visitor contact requires Scripture reading or prayer.* But do so if there is an opportunity.
9. *Keep all promises you make concerning confidentiality, help, or follow-up.*
10. *Tactfully confront sin, false teaching, or rumors.* Replace error with truth, always doing so with a loving spirit.

B. SPECIFIC GUIDELINES

Being in the hospital is often a time of uneasiness and fear. People will often have deep concerns, even if they do not show them. Certain proved guidelines should be followed in order to be an encouragement to those hospitalized. Although it is true that each situation is unique, some basic facts should always be kept in mind.

1. *Dress nicely when visiting.*
2. *At the hospital do not enter the room if the door is closed.* Either check with the nurses' station or knock.
3. *Be friendly and open, but not frivolous or silly.*
4. *Do not sit on the bed.*
5. *Do not get too personal about the medical problem, and do not tell horror stories about someone with a similar problem.* However, try to let the patient know that you are trying to understand his situation.
6. *Talk about areas of common interest such as the weather, sports, hobbies, and friends.* Get the patient's mind out of the hospital.
7. *You do not need to give a gift to every person.* But if you do, keep it simple.
8. *If the patient is able and wants to, suggest a walk around the corridor or to the waiting room.* Ask if he has any needs you can help with.

9. *Normally limit your visit to about fifteen minutes.* Remember that he is in the hospital to recover.

10. *If possible, read or quote Scripture.* Some suggestions for this:

A favorite passage of the patient

A passage from your daily devotions

Comforting psalms such as Psalms 4, 8, 16, 18:1-3, 23, 27, 34, 37:3-7, 40, 42, 46, 68:4-6, 71:1-9, 86, 90, 91, 95-100, 118:1-7, 121, 136, 139:1-10, and 146:1-5

Other passages that can help and comfort: Philippians 4:4-8; 1 Peter 5:7; Isaiah 43:2; 2 Thessalonians 3:3; Isaiah 40; Philippians 4:13, 19; John 14:1-3; Romans 8:35-39; Colossians 3:15, and 1 Peter 4:12-13

11. *Pray with the patient.* If appropriate, hold his hand. Pray for his physical condition, his emotional well-being, and his family at home. (Do keep it short!)

12. *Visit those having surgery the evening before or early in the morning before surgery.* Always read with and pray for those going into surgery. You could, of course, simply quote Scriptures of comfort.

13. *When visiting family members of those going through surgery, be a listening ear, a servant, and a friend.* Pray and read, if possible. Stay for a longer period of time.

III. TYPES OF CONTACT MINISTRIES

It has been said of Jesus Christ that no one left His presence without experiencing a positive change in his life. That should be the goal of all contact ministries. It is the primary goal of personal contact to point people to Christ and to help them move closer to Him. There are a variety of ways for leaders to be involved in this caring/contact ministry. But we want to look at four basic types of contact ministries.

A. FELLOWSHIP CONTACTS

Biblical fellowship is the sharing of the believer's life, both successes and failures, and the sharing of the resources of one another. The Greek word for fellowship, *koinonia,* has the basic idea of the sharing of a common life. Biblical fellowship does not stop at superficial conversation but goes beyond that to the disclosing of needs, burdens, hopes, goals, hurts, and sharing resources. Biblical fellowship can take place in informal settings, as well as organized ministries such as small groups. Every church must provide for fellowship in its programs and ministries.

B. EVANGELISTIC CONTACTS

One major goal of contact ministries is to provide church leaders opportunities to present the gospel to unbelievers. The spiritual leader must take the initiative to make these contacts. In our previous study area the matter of evangelism was dealt with in some detail, and that does not need to be repeated here. However, church growth experts have observed that unbelievers are most responsive to the gospel of Christ when going through a time of change or crisis. Hospital calls, home visits, and meeting with the sick and bereaved often are fruitful evangelistic contacts.

When making contact for evangelistic outreach, be sensitive to the time and place. If possible, plan a time that is adequate for sharing the gospel, answering questions, and dealing with objections. If you can, seek a place that is as free from distractions and interruptions as possible. If the person receives Christ as Savior, spend extended time in follow-up and further discussion.

C. CRISIS CONTACTS

Obviously you cannot put crises on your calendar ahead of time. But the elder and deacon must develop the mindset of availability in such cases. Crisis situations provide unique opportunities for personal contact and significant ministry. An appropriate response to someone in crisis will always draw people together. Our closest friends are usually those with whom we have cried. In a crisis, don't wait for an invitation—go immediately. (Unless, of course, there is an overriding reason not to.)

When responding to a crisis, don't be concerned that you must have all the answers or reasons that the situation has occurred. Don't try to be an "answer man," ready with unending words of wisdom and profound advice. Rather go to be a warm and caring person. Your presence is usually more important that what you say. Do not be embarrassed by long silences. (Remember that Job's friends sat quietly for seven days with their hurting friend and probably did their best "counseling" during that time!) An arm around the shoulder or a hug is certainly appropriate at such times, giving needed physical affirmation. Offer assistance in whatever way you can, at the same time staying out of the way of medical or emergency personnel. Pray and read (or quote) Scripture if the opportunity presents itself. Be ready to excuse yourself and leave when the person is ready to be alone or if friends and family members have responded and the person desires to be with them. Be sensitive to the needs of those going through crisis. Some may want to be alone, whereas others wish to be surrounded with family and friends.

Follow-up contact should be made the next day and perhaps for several days after that. It is often during the following days when the initial shock has worn off and reality has set in that we will have oportunities for counsel or witness. At all times, beware of trite remarks or cliches. Timely biblical counsel can be meaningful, whereas cliches can be damaging since they give the impression of insensitivity. Answer questions and doubts as best you can. If you don't know how to respond, say so and seek advice from others who may have some insight or wise counsel.

C. HOSPITALITY CONTACTS

The fourth type of contact ministry is to provide hospitality. Contact ministries can be carried out in hospitals, restaurants, cars, and over the telephone. However, one of the most rewarding places for contact ministry is your own home.

According to 1 Timothy 3, the elder is to practice hospitality. All believers are exhorted to care for others, using their resources (Titus 3:13-14). Generously opening home and possessions to others is an important avenue of ministry. Hospitality can provide for basic needs of food, clothing, and shelter. But it can also provide for the need for acceptance, the need to be loved, the need to be esteemed, the need to feel safe and protected, and the need for human touch and conversation. People need to be pampered, to be hosted, to have others interested in them, and to be willing to share their lives with them. Hospitality does not have to be elaborate or expensive—the meal or the nice room is not as important as the message it proclaims: "You are a worthwhile person, and I am honored to share my home and my possessions with you." Hospitality is a ministry area that entire families can share; and, in fact, they must, for it to be successful. (Note: An excellent resource book on the subject of hospitality is *Open Heart, Open Home,* by Karen Mains.)

Church leaders are undershepherds of the flock of God and have a responsibility to be in contact with people. A leader who views himself as a policy and decision maker but not a shepherd has misunderstood badly his responsibility. It is safe to say that a leader who is not in contact regularly in "people ministry" will not make the best decisions for the flock and will not provide the best leadership for that local church. Leaders must reach out and touch (contact) others.

CONCLUDING ASSIGNMENT:

List the established programs/ministries in place in your church now that are directly related to the four basic areas of contact ministry.

_____

_____

_____

How involved is the church leadership in these ministries? _____

_____

How involved are you in these ministries? _____

_____

Which area(s) do you believe need greater attention by your church? _____

_____

_____

What might be one goal for your church for this next year in the area of contact ministries? (Note: Try to state this in the format of a goal that we considered in our second area of study.) _____

_____

_____

SESSION 3:
COUNSELING AND GUIDING

An important part of the shepherding ministry in the church is biblical counseling. To counsel simply means to give advice or guidance. For the one who shepherds God's flock, the foundation for this advice and guidance is the Word of God. Spiritual leaders have a valuable commodity that both believers and unbelievers need, and that is the life-changing power of the Word of God. Martin and Deidre Bobgan in their book *How to Counsel from Scripture* state: "Most people seeking help need the kind of counsel in which the Bible excels: how to live, how to relate to others, how to find meaning in life, how to know God, and how to be the kind of person God wants."[1]

People need to be able to see life from God's perspective. This kind of wisdom is essential in order to grapple successfully with the problems and complexities of life. The leader, who has a working knowledge of the Scriptures, will be able to assist others as he helps shed the light of God's wisdom on their questions and problems.

PREPARATORY ASSIGNMENT:

Review the following portions of Scripture, which deal with this needed wisdom, and answer the questions.

1. Read Proverbs 1:20–2:6. Where do wisdom and knowledge come from? _____

_____

How does one obtain wisdom? _____

_____

What four categories of people are mentioned in this section? _____

_____

_____

How did these people come to be in their particular category? _____

_____

What are some inevitable consequences of being in their particular category? _____

_____

What does this section of Proverbs reveal about the importance of God's wisdom in handling life? _____

_____

_____

1. Martin and Deidre Bobgan, *How to Counsel from Scripture* (Chicago: Moody, 1985), p. 5.

2. Read 1 Corinthians 1:18-25; 2:6-9. What is the wisdom of the world unable to do?

_____

_____

What is true of God's wisdom? _____

_____

_____

3. According to Jesus in Matthew 7:24-27, what two elements make a man wise?

_____

_____

What is it that reveals the difference between the wise and the foolish? _____

_____

From these Scriptures, what basic truths do you see revealed in regard to God's wisdom? _____

_____

_____

_____

In this session we want to discuss three basic matters related to biblical counseling: the qualifications, the presuppositions, and some practical suggestions.

I. QUALIFICATIONS FOR BIBLICAL COUNSELING

It is the tendency of many spiritual leaders to avoid counseling because they fear that they are not qualified to do so. Although it is true that some people have needs or problems that require certain kinds of trained assistance, it is also true that a believer in Christ who is knowledgeable in the Word of God is qualified to counsel others. Jay Adams, in *Competent to Counsel,* declares that "Christian counselors properly trained in the scriptures are competent to counsel."[2] Others have noted that "problems of living must be dealt with as spiritual problems with spiritual solutions."[3] The Bible was given to reveal God's nature, God's provision for man, and God's directives as to how man should live. Therefore, if man is experiencing problems in living, he will find answers in the Word of God.

Who then is qualified to counsel? First, a person must know Jesus Christ as Savior. Proverbs declares that the fear of the Lord is the starting point of wisdom. When a person has established a right relationship with God, he then can begin to see life from God's viewpoint. And he can assist others in seeing life from this viewpoint. Second, that believer in Christ must have a working knowledge of God's Word. This comes from diligent study. With these two qualifications, a believer can give good advice and sound direction to others. However, one must develop and strengthen these abilities with continued study and life experience.

2. Jay Adams, *Competent to Counsel* (Grand Rapids: Baker, 1970), p. 19.
3. Bobgan, *How to Counsel,* p. xv.

Jay Adams presents three qualifications for biblical counselors: goodness, knowledge, and wisdom.[4] This comes from Romans 15:14, which states, "I myself am convinced, my brothers, that you yourselves are full of goodness, complete in knowledge and competent to instruct [counsel] one another."

Goodness in this verse is a noun referring to moral quality and a desire to be and to do good. The adjective form of the word emphasizes being morally honorable. One who is a biblical counselor should strive for personal holiness (goodness) and desire to do good or be of benefit to others.

Knowledge means the act of knowing. There are certain things that we must know. Any counseling requires a body of knowledge. The Scriptures are the body of knowledge needed by the biblical counselor. Therefore, to prepare for counseling, the biblical counselor must take every opportunity to know the Word of God.

Wisdom is also needed by the biblical counselor. Paul, in Colossians 3:16, says, "Let the word of Christ dwell in you richly as you teach and admonish [counsel] one another with all wisdom." Having wisdom assumes that a person has knowledge (facts and information). Wisdom is the ability to take knowledge and apply it to life's situations. Wisdom comes from the Word of God and from life experience. The believer is greatly enabled by the ministries of the Holy Spirit. The Holy Spirit has given the believer the capacity to understand the truth and gives divine assistance in difficult situations. James 1:5 says, "If any of you lack wisdom, he should ask God, who gives generously to all without finding fault, and it will be given to him."

The Holy Spirit helps the believer take previously studied truth and see its relevance and application to life. This wedding of God's truth to life situations provides that needed divine assistance enabling the leader to give wise counsel.

As the church tries to determine who in its ranks can be an effective counselor, it should look for some of the main qualifications or characteristics given in the book *How to Counsel from Scripture.*[5]

1. A believer who has a saving knowledge of the Lord Jesus Christ and who is living under His Lordship (following His teachings and commands).

2. A mature believer, who has known the Lord and relied on the indwelling Holy Spirit for some time. One who has allowed the Lord Jesus to be formed in him.

3. A believer who knows the Bible well, who knows how to apply the Scriptures in his own life, and who will counsel according to the Bible. Unless the counselor knows the Bible, he will counsel from worldly knowledge and experience.

4. A believer who has shown consistency, dependability, and responsibility in other work in the church.

5. A believer who is able to keep confidences.

6. A believer who is able to listen, to love, and to teach; one who is gifted in maintaining the balance of exhortation, teaching, and mercy, according to Romans 12.

7. A believer who follows his or her scriptural role in the home and whose home is in order. If a counselor is experiencing too many problems of his

4. Adams, *Competent to Counsel,* p. 62.
5. Bobgan, *How to Counsel,* pp. 184-85.

own, he will not be able to adequately bear the burdens of others in counseling.

8. A believer who relies on the Holy Spirit and who is faithful to pray for those he counsels. One who believes that God guides and directs His children and answers prayer.

9. A believer who does not intimidate, manipulate, or control others.

10. A believer who will not encourage those he counsels to become dependent on him.

II. PRESUPPOSITIONS FOR BIBLICAL COUNSELING

Every counselor uses a methodology in his/her counseling practice. This methodology is based on certain presuppositions or absolutes that the counselor believes to be true. This is also true of the biblical counselor. Note several basic biblical presuppositions.

A. THE BIBLE IS GOD'S INSPIRED WORD, WITHOUT ERROR, AND IS OUR ABSOLUTE STANDARD FOR FAITH AND PRACTICE.

The foundation for biblical counseling is the Word of God. If a biblical counselor has doubts about its truthfulness, then his ability to counsel effectively will be greatly reduced. He will lack confidence in both identifying the problem and in offering solutions.

INTERMEDIATE ASSIGNMENT: Memorize, and be ready to give from memory, the following two verses, which emphasize the critical importance of the Scriptures.

> All scripture is God-breathed and is useful for teaching, rebuking, correcting and training in righteousness, so that the man of God may be thoroughly equipped for every good work. (2 Tim. 3:14-17)

> For the word of God is living and active. Sharper than any double edged sword, it penetrates even to dividing soul and spirit, joints and marrow; it judges the thoughts and attitudes of the heart. (Heb. 4:12)

B. MAN AND CREATION ARE AFFECTED BY SIN.

One emphasis in our study of evangelism was that an unbeliever must come to a proper view of sin and its wages. In counseling, both counselor and counselee must recognize the effect of sin on all of creation. Sin has had a terrible effect on mankind. Sin has affected man's mind, his emotions, and his body. It has caused problems in man's relationships with God and with others. Therefore, in biblical counseling it is important to deal with individual sins, the sins of others, the sins of society, and the effects of sin on creation.

In dealing with problems of living, the believer still has to face the reality of sin, because sin is the ultimate source of all such problems. Some problems may not actually be due to a person's own disobedience to God, but all problems do come from living in a sinful world. Problems come from both sinning and being sinned against.

6. Ibid., p. 51.

Jesus Christ came to deal with the problem of sin. He paid the price for sin, and he came to bring restoration to those alienated by sin. When He returns, He will deal with the effects of sin on creation. A biblical counselor must point to Christ as the remedy for the problems of sin. The counselee must forgive those who have sinned against him, and he must confess and claim God's forgiveness for his own sin.

C. THE HOLY SPIRIT IS THE SUPREME COUNSELOR.

Jesus spoke of this role of the Spirit the night before His crucifixion. The Spirit has a unique ministry during counseling to both the counselor and the counselee.

When the Counselor comes, whom I will send to you from the Father, the Spirit of truth who goes out from the Father, He will testify about me. (John 15:26)

Unless I go away, the Counselor will not come to you, but if I go, I will send him to you. When He comes, He will convict the world of guilt in regard to sin and righteousness and judgment. (John 16:7-8)

But when He, the Spirit of truth, comes, He will guide you into truth. . . . He will bring glory to me by taking from what is mine and making it known to you. (John 16:13-14)

The counselor needs the ministry of the Holy Spirit directing his thoughts, his listening, and his spoken advice. Before and after the counseling session it is vital to pray for the ministry of the Spirit in the lives of those being counseled. As in the ministry of evangelism, at least three persons are involved in counseling: the counselor, the counselee, and the Holy Spirit. The counselor must be faithful in doing his part, recognizing that only the Holy Spirit can bring about true change.

D. BIBLICAL COUNSELING IS THE PRESENTATION OF THE PRINCIPLES AND PRACTICE OF THE SCRIPTURES.

Paul gave a formula for change when he stated that believers are to put off their old ways and put on the new by the renewing of their minds (Eph. 4:22-24). It is the task of biblical counseling to assist the individual in changing sinful habits into righteous habits by applying the principles of the Scriptures. A warning is in order, however. Some approach the Bible as though it were some sort of spiritual pharmacy that dispenses spiritual pills as the instantaneous remedy for all problems. Of course, the Bible does have the answers for the needs of mankind, but it is not "one verse for this problem and another verse for that." When engaged in biblical counseling, sound methods of biblical interpretation must be employed, such as interpreting the Scriptures in context and understanding cultural implications. Biblical counseling is based on biblical principles, not on proof texts.

E. THE GOAL OF BIBLICAL COUNSELING IS TO LEAD PEOPLE TO MATURITY IN CHRIST THROUGH CHANGE.

"We proclaim Him, admonishing and teaching everyone with all wisdom, so that we may present everyone perfect in Christ" (Col. 1:28). To become perfect in Christ requires change. Counseling deals with false thinking, sinful behavior, unrealistic expectations, ignorance, and problems of living. Almost without exception biblical counseling must emphasize the necessity of change. Biblical counseling works with the Holy Spirit in the sanctification of God's people.

F. BIBLICAL COUNSELING HOLDS A PERSON ACCOUNTABLE FOR HIS ACTIONS.

God has given man a free will. Therefore, God holds people accountable for their thoughts, words, and actions. Other methods of counseling will dismiss guilt as a figment of the imagination or will shift blame to society and others. Biblical counseling says: "Others may have sinned against you, but you are responsible and accountable for your actions. Will your situation control you, or will you, with God's help, control your situation?"

III. SUGGESTIONS FOR BIBLICAL COUNSELING

Many counseling books contain helpful suggestions and ideas. A few practical suggestions are given here that will help make a counseling ministry more effective.

A. LISTEN BEFORE YOU SPEAK.

Proverbs 18:13 declares that "he who answers before listening, that is his folly and his shame."

Some counselors believe they must do all the talking. But it is obvious that solutions cannot be given until the problem is known. The counselor must be an active listener and develop his listening skills. Active listening actually requires a great deal of energy. It is important really to hear the individual in order to ask good questions and be sensitive to the feelings behind the words.

B. GIVE PERTINENT ASSIGNMENTS.

Assignments help provide a remedy for problems and place a great deal of responsibility for change on the counselee. They quickly reveal how serious the counselee is in regard to bringing change into his life. Assignments may include reading a significant book in the area of the counselee's need or appropriate Scripture portions. They may include making restitution or not doing certain things. Memorization of Scripture or joining a small group might be assigned. There are many possibilities. Just be careful not to overload the individual.

C. REFER SITUATIONS TO OTHERS IF NECESSARY.

Since we are all limited in one way or another, it is no shame to admit lack of expertise in certain counseling situations and to refer counselees to others. We may lack the time to handle a counseling situation. Whatever the cause, refer counselees with grace and tact to others.

D. BE AWARE THAT SOME MENTAL AND EMOTIONAL PROBLEMS HAVE PHYSICAL CAUSES.

It may be wise to advise some counselees to have a physical examination. Counseling books give certain signs to look for in such instances.

E. WORK TO ATTRACT PEOPLE TO JESUS CHRIST AND NOT TO YOURSELF.

Counseling can be satisfying to the ego of the counselor. However, the biblical counselor must emphasize that healing and change can come only through a relationship with the Lord Jesus Christ and not with the counselor.

111

F. BE SENSITIVE TO INFORMAL COUNSELING OPPORTUNITIES.

Much of our counseling takes place in social gatherings, fellowship times, worship services, and group Bible studies. One reason lay counselors are effective is that they deal with the situation without a lot of time delays—at the present moment instead of at some future appointment. Be sensitive to counseling situations at unexpected times. Also be aware that much counseling takes place within the "body life" of the church, including the times of teaching and preaching.

G. EMPHASIZE PRAYER IN YOUR COUNSELING.

Before the counseling time, pray for wisdom. Pray with the counselee regarding his problem. And pray after the counseling time as a follow-up ministry.

H. ENGAGE IN SCRIPTURE MEMORIZATION.

It is helpful to have portions of the Word committed to memory. This can be one of the greatest assets of the biblical counselor.

SOME QUESTIONS TO CONSIDER:

In light of this study, what do you feel are the greatest strengths and weaknesses that you would bring into a counseling situation? _____

_____

_____

_____

It has been observed by secular researchers that "the personal qualities of the counselors are far more important than other factors, such as techniques and training."[7] Why would this be especially true for you as a biblical counselor?

_____

_____

_____

_____

_____

Who is doing the counseling in your church? _____

_____

What one goal would you set for this area of counseling in your church or in your personal life? _____

_____

_____

7. Ibid., p. 80.

SESSION 4:
EXPECTATIONS AND DISCIPLING

One priority of New Testament ministry is that of bringing others to the place of spiritual maturity. Paul instructed his own son in the faith, Timothy, to do for others what Paul had done for him.

> And the things which you have heard from me in the presence of many witnesses, these entrust to faithful men, who will be able to teach others also. (2 Tim. 2:2, NASB)

This, of course, is the fulfillment of Christ's command to "go and make disciples." Making disciples was a key element of the Lord's earthly ministry, and He wishes to carry on that ministry today through each of us.

PREPARATORY ASSIGNMENTS:

As we enter this subject area it is helpful to review some pertinent Scripture passages that deal with the matter of discipleship. The gospel records give us some insights about Christ's discipleship ministry.

1. Read the following Scriptures and note the expectations and requirements the Lord Jesus had for those who would be His disciples: Matthew 12:46-49; 19:27-29; Luke 9:23-26; 9:57-62; 17:7-10.

_____

_____

_____

_____

_____

2. In the following Scriptures we find many of the elements that were a part of Christ's discipling of His disciples. What are they? Matthew 5:1-3; 10:1-7; 17:1-7; 19:27; 24:3; 26:33-45; John 6:5-12.

_____

_____

_____

_____

_____

3. From your investigation of these Scripture portions, what do you believe to be the key elements in making good, solid disciples? _____

_____

_____

_____

In this session we want to focus on the issues "Who is a disciple?" and "How we make disciples?" We will also relate discipling to "discipline."

I. THE MINISTRY OF DISCIPLESHIP

A. WHO IS A DISCIPLE?

1. *Defining the term.* Discipleship is a buzz word in Christian circles. But it has been used and misused so much that there is a lack of clarity as to what it actually means. Are all believers disciples? Just when does a person become a disciple? Are there varying degrees of discipleship? The New Testament refers to disciples of John the Baptist, Moses, the Pharisees, and, of course, the Lord Jesus. So a variety of people had disciples. The word "disciple" comes from the Greek word *mathetes* and fundamentally refers to a person who is an apprentice, pupil, or learner. In its usage it basically meant a follower of another. However, the commitment level of that follower to the teacher and the teacher's precepts was not clear. There could have been a high level of commitment or almost no commitment. In this study, however, we will define a disciple of Jesus Christ as one who has a high level of commitment to the Person of the Lord Jesus and to the truths of the Christian faith as presented in the Word of God.

It is interesting to note that this ambiguity in the word "disciple" apparently caused the writers of the New Testament epistles to abandon the use of the word. They, for example, did not refer to themselves as disciples of the Lord Jesus. Instead they used the term "bondslave" (Greek word *doulos*). A bondslave had no rights of his own and was completely under the will of his master. There was no ambiguity in "bondslave." However, this concept of a bondslave is essentially the idea that we want to have as we use the words "disciple" and "discipleship." We are looking at people who have submitted themselves and committed themselves to the Lord Jesus Christ.

2. *Christ's definition of discipleship.* In Luke 9:23-26 and 14:25-33, we find Christ's definition of discipleship. Apparently Jesus was disturbed by those who were following Him just because of His popularity, miracles, and authoritative teaching. Jesus wanted disciples, not shallow followers. In these verses the Lord gave several aspects of discipleship.

a. A desire to be a disciple. Jesus declared that "if anyone wishes to come after me" then there were certain things that must be true. But discipleship had to be the desire of the heart of an individual. This was the starting point. The Lord Jesus never coerced or manipulated people into the ranks of discipleship. There was (and is) no hope of a person's being a genuine disciple if he did not desire to be one.

b. A surrender of one's own rights. Basic to following Christ is the willingness to let Him lead. A true disciple turns over the reins of his life to Jesus Christ. It is a vow, a lifetime commitment. This was and is serious. That is why Jesus never forced people to follow Him and even raised issues that caused them to turn away from following Him (cf. Luke 9:57-62). He made clear that there could be no competition for loyalty. Those who would be His disciples had to "hate" anything that would hold them back from total obedience to Him. The question is, "Who is number one in our lives?"

c. An identification each day with Christ. A cross symbolized death. To take up our cross is to die to our ways and desires and identify ourselves with His ways and desires. Note that this is a daily issue. How do we live on a daily basis? Basically we identify with Christ by living a biblical lifestyle—by living godly in an ungodly world. Our speech, standards of behavior, and our attitudes reflect our relationship with Christ and promote Him, not ourselves. The question is, "Does my lifestyle accurately reflect the fact that I am a follower of Jesus Christ?"

d. A willingness to pay any cost. The Lord taught clearly that there is a cost to discipleship and that each individual must count the cost. A commitment to Christ means that we wave good-bye to everything of importance—to possessions, family, goals, and desires. This does not mean the Master will require that they be abandoned. But it does mean that the issue of our loyalty is settled. This is where our greatest struggles occur. And sometimes we need the help of the Lord Himself actually to "give up" these valuable things and people. The prayer of A. W. Tozer reflects the heart condition of most of us and yet the willingness to be changed by God's power and grace:

> Father, I want to know thee, but my coward heart fears to give up its toys. I cannot part with them without inward bleeding, and I do not try to hide from thee the terror of the parting. I come trembling, but I do come. Please root from my heart all those things which I have cherished so long and which have become a very part of my living self, so that thou mayest enter and dwell there without a rival. . . . Amen.[1]

The end result will probably be that certain cherished things of life (some good in and of themselves) must be set aside. But it must be remembered that the Lord Jesus is a kind and loving Master who will always seek what is the best for His disciples.

It should be noted that several times the Lord Jesus declared that a person who would not do these things just mentioned in our study could not be His disciple.

SOME QUESTIONS TO CONSIDER:

Before one can disciple others, he must first be a disciple of Christ himself. Would you consider yourself a disciple? _____

Of the four aspects of Christ's definition of discipleship, which one have you struggled with the most? _____

_____

_____

1. A. W. Tozer, *The Pursuit of God* (Harrisburg, Pa.: Christian Publications, 1958), p. 131.

Was there any particular point in time when you believe you really "joined the ranks" of Jesus' disciples? Could you share that?

_____

_____

Although there has been an emphasis on "giving up" to be Christ's disciple, much is gained. In your experience, what have been the greatest benefits in your life since you became a true disciple of Christ?

_____

_____

B. HOW ARE DISCIPLES MADE?

Christ not only commanded us to "go and make disciples," but He modeled how to produce them. Mark 3:13-14 and Luke 9:23-27; 57-62 provide several clues as to how Christ carried out the process of discipleship.

1. *Christ selected carefully those He discipled.* Discipleship does not take place between strangers. Discipleship involves a special relationship. When Christ chose His twelve apostles out of a much larger group of disciples, He took the initiative and called them to Himself. One who is serious about the ministry of discipleship will be alert for individuals who demonstrate interest in the things of Christ. It is in this kind of person that leaders should invest their time and energy.

A good place to start is with those whom the spiritual leader has led to the Lord. Remember that evangelism involves providing for the maturity of the converts. It is a special privilege to disciple one's own spiritual children. Other potential candidates could be new believers with whom a friendly relationship has already been established. Also, if a leader has children, these children should be primary objects of discipling. Discipleship may be done one-on-one or in small groups.

The establishment of a discipleship relationship must be voluntary for all parties involved. We must be sensitive to the Lord's leadership because we do not want to force people into a discipling relationship. It is important to spend time in prayer, as Jesus Himself did before selecting the Twelve (Luke 6:12-16). One note of caution: Because of the potential for intimacy in discipleship, it is important that men disciple men and women disciple women.

2. *Christ spent time with those He discipled.* Far too often when one thinks of discipleship the focus is on curriculum, that is, on a body of truth or information that must be passed on. Content is, of course, important. But the Lord emphasized relationship over content.

The uniqueness of discipleship is that teaching and training can be tailored and customized to the maturity level of those being discipled. An infant is fed with milk; an adult is fed with meat. The discipler may find it helpful to have a lesson plan and topics listed that he wishes to discuss. But as time is spent with an individual, issues and problems may come up that were unseen initially. The beauty of discipleship is that the Holy Spirit may direct that all plans be set aside to deal with another question or problem. Through prayer we must be sensitive to the direction of the Spirit.

One benefit of emphasizing relationship over content is better accountability. Those who know each other well can hold each other accountable much easier than those who are more distant.

3. *Christ discipled so that they might minister.* Christ's goal of discipleship was not to keep His twelve men perpetually dependent on Him but to send them out to carry on His ministry. There needs to be a termination point for all discipleship relationships. The purpose of discipleship is not to create followers of ourselves but of Jesus Christ. For three years Christ prepared His disciples for the time He would leave them. The goal of discipleship is to train "reliable men who will also be qualified to teach others."

Once again, be sensitive to the leading of the Holy Spirit through prayer as to when the termination of the discipling relationship should take place. Some set a date for termination when they begin. Others set a goal to reach and then terminate when the goal is reached. Still others are more subjective, simply terminating the relationship at a mutually agreed-upon time when it seems the process is completed.

The termination of a discipling relationship does not mean the end of all social contact and interaction. On the contrary, close friendships are often formed in discipleship and continue long after the process comes to an end.

SOME QUESTIONS TO CONSIDER:

It has been said that everyone needs a Paul (someone older and wiser to help us in our Christian walk), a Barnabas (someone who is our equal and to whom we can be accountable), and a Timothy (someone whom we can teach and train). As you think about your Christian walk over the years, who has been in those roles for you?

My Paul(s) _____

My Barnabas(s) _____

My Timothy(s) _____

Is there anyone whom you are presently discipling? _____

Is there anyone whom you think you should be discipling? _____

If you are not discipling anyone presently, would you make this possibility a matter of prayer?

II. THE MINISTRY OF DISCIPLINE

Sometimes a needed part of shepherding the flock is corrective discipline. The word *discipline* basically means "training." Training can include both positive teaching or negative correction. When we think of discipling people, we normally think in terms of having positive input into their lives as we try to bring them along the road to spiritual maturity. It is also true that discipleship sometimes involves the need to confront, warn, and correct. (Note some of that in Paul's epistles.) Although this session has emphasized the shepherding (discipline) of newer converts, we must broaden the discussion of corrective discipline beyond these individuals to the church as a whole. In one sense, of course, the process of discipleship goes on continually in the lives of all God's people in our church.

At this point, read several key New Testament passages that deal with the subject of corrective discipline: 1 Corinthians 5:1-11; 2 Thessalonians 3:6-15; Galatians 6:1; Acts 20:28-30; and Matthew 18:15-17.

A. THE SUBJECTS OF DISCIPLINE

All believers, in one sense, have a responsibility to deal with sinful behavior. Yet it is to the spiritually mature believer that the Scriptures give the task of dealing with difficult and complex situations. The leader, then, has the responsibility to see that needed discipline takes place. Elders and deacons have God-given authority in the church, and it needs to be exercised in these situations. This authority has been granted primarily to build up and strengthen the church (2 Cor.13:1). But, in cases where sin is a major concern, the authority of these leaders can be exercised to deal with that sin.

B. THE PURPOSE OF DISCIPLINE

Discipline has the goal of restoration, not judgment or condemnation. Discipline is designed to alert the sinning believer to the foolishness of his ways and, through the Word of God, to enlighten him to the reality of his situations and the sure consequences of sin. The process of discipline is intended to bring about godly sorrow, restoration, and advancement in his Christian life.

Discipline also must be carried out in order to purify the church. The health and well-being of others will be affected by discipline or the lack of it. Also, the discipline of an individual acts as a deterrent to sin in the church at large.

C. THE REASONS FOR DISCIPLINE

Church discipline is not to be exercised in the case of every sin or deviation from the truth. Church discipline is not God's method of making the church sinless. Leaders would spend their entire waking moments exercising discipline if every single sin committed were to be dealt with. The Scriptures do, however, give guidelines as to what constitutes a disciplinary offense. It should be obvious that any sin that does damage to the church, weakens its testimony, or promotes disunity must be dealt with. And any sin that has a clear *potential* for hurting the church must be addressed. Some specific sins mentioned in the New Testament must be addressed (e.g., Gal. 1:6-8; Acts 20:28-30; 2 Thess. 3:11; Titus 3:10-11; 2 Thess. 3:6, 14; 1 Cor. 5:11; Phil. 4:2-3; 1 Cor. 6:5).

D. THE PROCESS OF DISCIPLINE

Any time that sin can be properly dealt with in a private setting the better off the church is, since younger believers and carnal believers do not do well with the sins of others. Matthew 18:15-17 and Titus 3:10-11 give guidelines on the process of discipline. First, the sinning believer is confronted privately and personally with the Word of God. Church discipline actually begins at this stage (whatever else may have preceded it), when there is recognition of an offense that threatens, or has already hurt, the purity of the church. To ensure the accuracy of reports and to make sure that the general procedure of Matthew 18 is carried out, one mature, knowledgeable leader should confront the sinning believer with the truth of God. If there is repentance the procedure stops at that point.

If the leader's efforts fail, witnesses are to be taken along as another attempt is made to restore the sinning believer. These witnesses (probably other mature leaders) will be the basis for bringing the case before a larger group if no repentance occurs.

If there is no repentance at that point, then the instruction is to "tell it to the church." The purpose of so doing is to shame the sinning believer and to put godly pressure on him from the concerned, praying Christian community. If he still does not repent, he is to be removed from the life of the church and viewed as an unbeliever.

E. THE ATTITUDE IN DISCIPLINE

When one sins and resists the disciplinary process, there is a general tendency for the leadership to become harsh and proud. The Scriptures exhort those who discipline to be careful about their attitudes. They are not to be proud, thinking that they are strong and superior. They are to treat the sinning believer as a brother and not as an enemy. They are to mourn over this success of Satan. There should always be a readiness to forgive.

F. THE RESPONSE TO DISCIPLINE

When a believer acknowledges the seriousness of his sin, demonstrates a godly sorrow, and confesses it to God and men (since men have now become involved), then forgiveness and restoration to full fellowship is to take place. (Note that they may not necessarily be restored to ministry, however.) It is the responsibility of the leaders to determine if genuine godly sorrow and repentance has occurred. In some cases, restitution may be necessary. Restitution may be significant in demonstrating the genuineness of a person's repentance. When godly sorrow "which leads to repentance" takes place, the repentant one is to have special care and encouragement from the church to keep him from being "swallowed up with overmuch sorrow" (2 Cor. 2:7, KJV).

Church discipline is never easy, and it is never an enjoyable aspect of shepherding. But it is an obligation given by the Lord to the church. Leaders do not need to go out looking for discipline cases, but if they shepherd faithfully over the years they will encounter situations that call for discipline. This is not a pleasant task, but one that must be done for the sake of the church and the sinning believer.

SOME QUESTIONS TO CONSIDER:

Does your church have a written position on the matter of church discipline? _____

If it does, are the members of your church generally aware of its existence and do they have access to it? _____

If not, is there a plan to get such a document written soon? _____

What kinds of disciplinary offenses do you believe most leaders should expect to encounter in the church today? _____

_____

_____

What do you think are the main reasons most churches do not enter into the process of church discipline, even though offenses that need discipline are in the church?

_____

_____

_____

_____

A FINAL THOUGHT TO CONSIDER:

When David was being pursued by King Saul, he needed help. He did not just need warriors, he needed leaders. First Chronicles 12:32 (NASB) states that he found leaders: "Of the sons of Issachar, men who understood the times, with knowledge of what Israel should do."

The church today needs such men. May you be that kind of person in the ministry where God has placed you.